Would You Think and Do Things Differently if You Were a Millionaire?

Dear Reader,

Have you ever driven by a truly magnificent home and instantly fallen in love with it? Did it make you wonder what the owner did for a living? "How could they possibly afford such an expensive property?" you may have lamented.

Perhaps you just shrugged your shoulders and said, "Well, he's probably a doctor, a lawyer, or a business owner. It sure would be nice to be able to afford something like that, but we're just regular people." With a tear in your eye, you drive away, dismissing the idea of ever of owning such a beautiful property.

But wait a minute!

Who said you can't be wealthy, have the home of your dreams, and live like those people do? Where is it written? Who decides who lives in what kind of house and where, anyway? Are they any better than you? Do they deserve it more than you? Do they know something you don't know?

Have you ever asked how and what they think?

Did you grow up believing that all you needed to do was get a good education and a good job with good benefits, and you'd be set for life? That's exactly what most people have done, but it didn't create for them the lives they really wanted. Instead, they got deeper in debt and stressed out, and don't really like their jobs—for one reason or another. Many even blamed others for their situation.

But it doesn't have to be that way!

So Why Aren't More People More Successful?

First of all, let's define success. Ask anyone who has achieved outstanding success and they're likely to tell you that it's the *progressive* realization of a worthwhile dream, goal, or objective. But they'll also tell you it's more than that—good health, peace of mind, caring relationships, personal fulfillment, and financial freedom. Success is a journey, not a destination. It's not an end point. The journey *is* the success! It's a lifelong process—a continuum.

Some people think that when they attain this or that, then they'll be successful and happy; they will have arrived. The trouble is, when they get there, it may be great for a little while, but the feeling always goes away. It's as if something were missing—and it is! We're like fruit that's ripe. When it stops growing, it starts to rot. We're either progressing or falling behind. Maintaining the status quo really means we're losing ground because time is marching on.

There are some basic truths that determine the degree to which people succeed. First of all, if we want to be more successful, we need to wholeheartedly embrace the idea—the *thought*—of being more successful. No one else can do our thinking for us.

Have you ever heard anyone say they're a victim of circumstances? While, at times, this may appear to be the case, the true champions in life don't use circumstances to excuse themselves from accomplishing things. They rise above their circumstances. They know they are totally responsible for their lives, and they take charge.

Achieving ongoing success requires continuous properly directed thinking and effective use of our minds, at which most people, unfortunately, are woefully unskilled. Most people's thinking is not proactive, but more like background activity and mostly reactive. Instead of being focused on getting better results, they expend much of their time and energy "putting out fires." They're like a hamster running in a caged wheel—working like crazy but getting nowhere. Most people think semiconsciously nearly all the time, operating out of habit. They think the same old thoughts, do the same old things, and, therefore, keep getting the same old results. Their attention is undisciplined and not sharply focused on what they want. But success isn't going to be handed to us. Our quest must be deliberate and sustained.

So how can this be done?

Change Your Thinking and You'll Change Your Life!

Have you ever wondered why most hardworking people never seem to get ahead or really accomplish much of any significance? Have you noticed that this scenario generally continues for the rest of their lives? Have you also noticed that there are some people who don't seem to work hard at all, yet they're always on top of the world? They keep having success after success throughout their lives, and always seem to have smiles on their faces. Doesn't this remind you of the expression, "The rich get richer and the poor get poorer"?

But why is that?

How people live and what they accomplish is primarily the result of their thinking—and the actions they take based on those thoughts. Once a thought or idea enters the mind, the mind is forever changed. As the Scriptures say, "As a man thinketh, so is he." When that thought or idea is acted upon, the person's life is also forever changed.

Once you think a new thought about improving your life and take action on it, you immediately start living at a higher level. From then on, your new level of awareness tells you anything less is undesirable. You're no longer able to accept the status quo. Maybe that's why you're reading this book. You've had quite enough of the way things have been going and you've chosen to improve your situation.

Will your boss help you do that?

This Book Won't Help You Either, Unless...

...you're willing to take action on what it teaches. No! Let me rephrase that. It won't help you one iota unless you *actually* take action. Just being *willing* to take action won't cut it. You *must* take action! When you do, your life will start changing, and one positive thing will lead to another. When successful people don't like the way something is, they change it. They don't wallow in self-pity; they don't whine or complain; and they don't make excuses. They get on with it.

The purpose of *The Parable of the Homemade Millionaire* is to teach you how to use your mind more effectively, and encourage you to find a mentor or leader—so you can create the life you want—sooner rather than later. These ideas have been used by the most successful people in the world, including many who conduct their businesses from the comfort of their own homes. But they won't impact your life until you start applying them, while building relationships with people who are where you want to be—people who have created a lifestyle that supports doing what's on their hearts to do. After all, you become like the people you associate with.

Welcome to the neighborhood of homemade millionaires!

All things grow with love,

The Publisher

PS. This is one of the most compelling manuscripts we've ever published. Apply and share its life-enhancing, to-the-core-of-success secrets with others, and you, too, could become a homemade millionaire.

The Parable

—of the—

Homemade Millionaire

Now Anyone Can Wake the
Millionaire Within and Discover
the Opportunity of a Lifetime

Bryan James

Foreword by Charlie "Tremendous" Jones

A Book

The Parable
—of the—
Homemade Millionaire

Now Anyone Can Wake the
Millionaire Within and Discover
the Opportunity of a Lifetime

Bryan James

Copyright © 2006 by Possibility Press & Bryan James
ISBN 0-938716-64-6

1   2   3   4   5   6   7   8   9   10

Published by *Possibility Press*
info@possibilitypress.com

Manufactured in the United States of America

Dedication

To everyone with the wisdom and courage to create a better life by following the guidance of those who have... and then sharing it with others.

Acknowledgment

Thanks to my loving wife, Jeanne, who encouraged me to write this book to help others.

I thank God, for without him, this book would not have been possible. I thank Him for helping me not only go through but, more importantly, grow through so many challenges in business and in life. He molded me so I could share more effectively with others and, hopefully, make a bigger difference. Maybe you'll allow Him to do the same for you.

A special thank you to the staff at Possibility Press for believing in me, and sharing my passion for helping others succeed. Their relentless creative, editorial, and design work resulted in more than I could have ever imagined. Without them, this book would not exist.

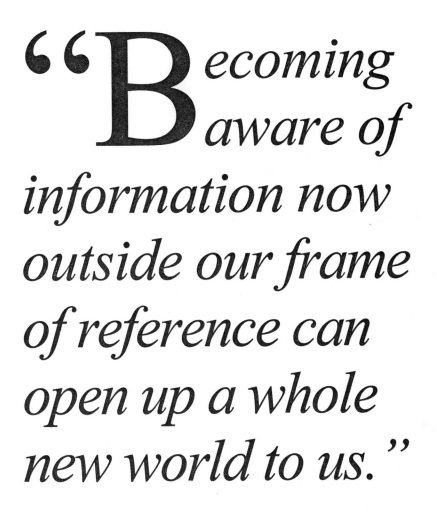

"Becoming aware of information now outside our frame of reference can open up a whole new world to us."

—Zors

Contents

A Tremendous Message!

In *The Parable of the Homemade Millionaire*, Bryan James gives us a sterling example of the potential that lies within us all—and how it can be nurtured by a caring mentor and friend.

This exciting little book shares a BIG liberating message that teaches us how to rise above the hum-drum everydayness of the workaday world. It illustrates that great opportunity can be found in the books we read and the people we meet.

As I've experienced, you'll be the same in five years as you are today except for the books you read and the people you meet. The person who shared this book with you could be someone like Zors, the Homemade Millionaire, or lead you to someone like him. Keep this in mind as you read the story. This person could open up a whole new exciting world to you, and you could make the positive changes you want in life just like Jonathan, Zors' mentee, did.

If you want some things to change in your life, you need to change some things in your life! So start using the life-changing ideas in this great little book to build a better life for yourself and your family— you'll be glad you did.

Thank goodness you have the chance to read this tremendous book. Remember, life is tremendous when you seize a good opportunity and make the most of it

Tremendously,

Charlie "Tremendous" Jones
Speaker and Bestselling
Author of *Life Is Tremendous*

"*Associate yourself with people of good quality...for 'tis better to be alone than in bad company.*"

—George Washington

—Chapter 1—

Setting the Stage

I didn't know it at the time, but we were about to meet two of the most important people of our lives. On that crisp, beautifully sunny fall day, my wife, Jennifer, and I noticed new neighbors moving in. We were trying to imagine what they'd be like, but we never could have guessed how much our relationship with them would dramatically change our lives. We also didn't know that their choice of that particular property was not just a chance occurrence!

We were an average, hardworking couple with two kids, yearning for a better life. Like most people, we were slogging back and forth to work, putting our time in, looking forward to weekends, thinking we were doing okay. But all we could seem to do was barely make ends meet, while getting deeper in debt.

Like most people, we were taught that if we got good educations and good jobs with good benefits, we'd be set for life. But it just wasn't working out that way. After being on the job scene for over a decade, we honestly thought we'd be further ahead. Jennifer was a nurse and I was an editor at a publishing house. However, our jobs, and the stress that went along with them, had become quite frustrating. All of it was starting to get us down, and it was tiresome always having someone else tell us what to do.

As the middle-aged couple, Michael and Ruth Zors, moved in next door, Jennifer and I were curiously watching from our living room window. There were only a few initial clues telling us what kind of people they were, but it was obvious they were affluent. The house was somewhat secluded, surrounded by some of the most beautifully landscaped acreage you could ever imagine. It was also the biggest, nicest house in the neighborhood, and their furniture appeared substantial and elegant.

It didn't look like they had any children still living at home, but they were certainly young enough to be vital and actively productive. Before we could observe much more, however, the movers were done and the couple had disappeared into their new home. It wasn't until the following day that we would discover who they were.

"*Like most people, we were also taught that if we got good educations and good jobs with good benefits, we'd be set for life. But it just wasn't working out that way.... Our jobs, and the stress that went along with them, had become quite frustrating. All of it was starting to get us down, and it was tiresome always having someone else telling us what to do.*"

—Jonathan Weatherby

"The house is exactly what they were looking for. It's a very classy home, but not ostentatious. Zors is a pretty humble guy, even though I believe he probably has enough money to buy the entire town—and then some!"

—Mark Webster

—Chapter 2—

The First Meeting

The next day, we felt compelled to go next door and meet our new neighbors. A well-dressed woman who looked to be in her mid- to late-forties answered the door.

"Hello, we're your next-door neighbors, Jonathan and Jennifer Weatherby. Welcome to the neighborhood!" I offered, smiling.

She smiled back and extended her hand to shake ours, "Well, thank you very much. I'm Ruth Zors and it's nice to meet you. Please come in. I'll get my husband."

We were escorted into the living room, which seemed way too orderly for people who had just moved in the day before. Ruth left us alone and went to find her husband. In the short time Ruth was out of the room, Jennifer visually absorbed as much as possible. I was less interested in the surroundings, as I was trying to remember where I had heard the name Zors. Somewhere, in the back of my mind, I knew I had heard it before and had a good feeling about it. But I couldn't remember the details.

"Hello," her husband said suddenly, shaking me out of my contemplation, as he walked into the room. "I'm Michael

Zors, but everyone just calls me Zors. Ruth tells me you live next door."

"Yes, we're Jonathan and Jennifer Weatherby," I responded. After we shook hands, Jennifer handed Ruth the pie she had baked for them.

"It's apple," Jennifer said, beaming. "And it's homemade. We thought you'd enjoy it."

As Ruth was thanking us, Zors chimed in "Wait a minute, this pie is round. I thought *pie* are squared!"

Obviously this was a mathematical joke, but it caught us off guard. Finally, thinking this man's quite the intellect, and a comical one at that, we forced a chuckle as Ruth saved the moment.

"Don't mind him," she said, "he's had a weird sense of humor most of his life." Now we really laughed, and knew, somehow, that this was going to be a unique relationship.

"Well, we don't want to keep you," I said. "You probably have a lot of work to do and we've got to get going anyway. We're driving across town to visit some friends. And with my sense of direction, the trip could take all day!"

"Now that's an affirmation that will serve you well," Zors said with a laugh. "Well, it was kind of you to stop over. It's been great meeting you. I hope we'll get to spend more time with you."

"I'm sure we will," I responded. "Have a nice day."

As we left and started walking back to our house, I turned to Jennifer and asked, "Wasn't that a little strange?"

"What do you mean?" she said. "I thought they were nice."

"Yes, but what was that pie (pi) joke all about? Is this guy a brain or something—not to mention the affirmation that will serve you well?"

Before Jennifer could answer, we saw a familiar car pull into the Zors' circular driveway. Jennifer went back into the house to get ready to leave for our appointment. "Mark," I yelled as I walked towards him, "what are you doing here?"

"I'm here to see Zors."

Mark and Connie Webster were longtime friends of ours and, all of a sudden, seeing them reminded me of where I had heard the name *Zors*.

"Hold on a second. Is this the Zors you're in business with?" I asked. "Does he own the business you shared with me last year that I said 'no' to?"

"Sure," he laughed, "how do you think he knew this property was for sale?"

All at once, several questions went rushing through my brain, but I didn't know which to ask first. Before I opened my mouth, Mark continued, "When Connie and I were over at your house for dinner a while back, I noticed that this place was for sale, so I told Zors about it. How does it feel, so far, to live next to the smartest, kindest, most caring couple in the world?"

"In the world? What do you mean?" I asked, "Hold on a minute; I've got some questions for you!"

"Go ahead, but I'm in a little bit of a hurry though," he said.

"First of all, why would this guy move here? True, it's the nicest house in the neighborhood, but the owner of a huge international business could well afford something even bigger. And secondly, why do you think they're the smartest, kindest, most caring people in the world? I just met them and, frankly, I wasn't impressed. Actually, I thought he was a little offbeat. None of this makes any sense."

Mark was really smiling by now. "Reserve judgment on him for a while. When you get to know him, you'll understand."

"Fair enough, but why did they choose *this* particular property?" I asked.

"The house is exactly what they were looking for. It's a very classy home, but not ostentatious. Zors is a pretty humble guy, even though I believe he probably has enough money to buy the entire town—and then some! In fact, he and Ruth operate a charitable foundation to help those who can't afford expensive medical procedures."

"But why not show off a little? After all, he earned it. Why not enjoy his success?"

"Oh, he enjoys it alright," Mark said, "but it's always good to be humble and thankful for your success. That's how Zors is, anyway, and Ruth too."

"Well, Zors fascinates me the most, I've got to admit. What's he really all about?"

Mark looked pensive for a moment and finally said, "I don't think I could do him justice if I tried to explain him to you. You really need to get to know him yourself. All I'll say is that he has positively impacted my life in a big way. Believe me, your new neighbor and his wife are very special people. I would imagine you and Zors will see a fair amount of each other—that is, if you're as fortunate as I am."

"You really need to get to know him yourself. All I'll say is that he has positively impacted my life in a big way. Believe me, your new neighbor and his wife are very special people."

—Mark Webster

"**F**riendship is the only cement that will ever hold the world together."

—Woodrow Wilson

—Chapter 3—

Coming Together
as Friends

We didn't see much of the Zors couple in the weeks to come. We'd wave to them in passing, but they were always going somewhere or entertaining guests. Sometimes they'd have a dozen or more cars parked in front of their house. With all the activity, there weren't too many opportunities to really get to know them.

We lived in a quiet neighborhood where most people kept to themselves. We knew our other neighbors well enough to say hello, but little or nothing else about them. It seemed that everyone wanted it that way—until Zors moved in, that is.

It was very cold that November and most of the month we had snow and high winds. One night we were awakened suddenly by a loud crash. I leaped out of bed, ran to the window, and saw that a large tree had blown down across our backyard, barely missing the house. I was scared and relieved at the same time, but I knew I had to get that tree out of the yard.

The following Saturday, I resigned myself to the task at hand. Removing the tree was going to take all day, so I got as early a start as possible. But I didn't want to begin too early, as the chainsaw would surely wake the neighbors. So I began at 9 o'clock.

After about fifteen minutes, I looked up and was surprised to see Zors walking toward the other end of the tree. He never spoke or even looked at me; he just started working. Within a few minutes, Don, our next door neighbor from the other side of the house, joined us with his chainsaw. Before too long, other neighbors began joining in. I couldn't help but think that, by his example, Zors had shown all of us how to be better neighbors.

Within about two hours, the project was completed. The tree was reduced to firewood, which was meticulously piled at the edge of our wooded area. All the small limbs and branches were bound together with twine, ready to be used as kindling. I honestly didn't know where the twine had come from. Then, as quickly as they came, all the neighbors were gone and our yard was clean again. It had been a wonderful gift from the neighbors, initiated by our unique and mysterious new friend.

Somehow, that incident brought the neighborhood together. We began caring about and talking to each other and doing kind things for one another; we all became friends. Zors had quietly, unassumingly led the way. It was the first of many incredible lessons I would learn from this man—lessons that would change my life!

"We began caring about and talking to each other and doing kind things for one another; we all became friends. Zors had quietly, unassumingly led the way."

—Jonathan Weatherby

"**D**eep down inside, I'd had a gnawing feeling of dissatisfaction for quite some time, but I had just been ignoring it—thinking there was nothing I could do about it. All my friends seemed to be doing things the same way I was, and I thought this must be all there was to life. But now I was beginning to get a glimmer of hope...."

—Jonathan Weatherby

—Chapter 4—

What's Out There?

Shortly after the amazing tree-cutting experience, we invited Zors and his wife over for coffee. We felt it was important to acknowledge and thank him for his kindness, while it would give us the best opportunity to get to know them both better. I was very interested in discovering why Mark, personally, found this couple to be so brilliant and caring. But I wouldn't realize until later that Ruth, in her own right, was even more amazing than Zors!

Upon arrival, smiling, Zors handed us a bunch of bananas. "I stopped by the zoo earlier today, and the chief chimp handed me these," he quipped with a wink.

And that was just the beginning. For the next hour, we had a most delightful and entertaining conversation with these two thoroughly engaging people. Both Zors and Ruth were wonderful, loving people, and Zors was quite the comedian. Actually, he had a corny sense of humor, but knew exactly when and how to use it. I still, however, hadn't seen the brilliance to which Mark had alluded.

As we were finishing the conversation, Zors asked us about our hobbies and dreams. We shared that we would like to spend more time with the kids, other than shuffling them from one activity to another. We'd also like to play more golf, which we really enjoy. Zors then said his business had given him more time with his kids, then started talking about his love of golf. But his next comment was most curious.

"My game really improved when I went to a weaker grip, compliments of my internal receiver," he said.

The conversation continued as I resisted the urge to ask him what he was talking about. After a while, I couldn't stand it any longer.

As subtly and intelligently as I could muster, I asked, "You mentioned your 'internal receiver.' I don't believe I'm familiar with that terminology."

"Oh, I'm sorry," he replied. "It has to do with a methodology of opening up your awareness to information you need."

"I'm not already open to information I need?" I asked.

"Only if the information is important to you," Zors responded.

"I don't follow you," I said. "If I need information, then it *must* be important to me, right?" I noticed, out of the corner of my eye, Ruth had an ever-so-subtle smile on her face, and was trying to suppress a chuckle.

"If you knew it was important to you," Zors responded. "Let me give you an example. How many pairs of brown shoes have you seen today?"

"What?" I said, not understanding where he was coming from or what he was talking about.

"Brown shoes. You know, what people wear on their feet. How many pairs did you see today?"

"I don't know," I said. I felt I was getting set up for a joke and wasn't sure I liked it.

"Of course you don't know. But do you know why you don't know?" Zors asked.

"I guess I don't care," I said defensively, not wanting to be the butt of a joke.

"That's right!" he exclaimed. "It doesn't mean anything to you, does it? But now let's say I spend the day with you tomorrow, and pay you a hundred dollars for every pair of brown shoes you point out to me. You'd notice every pair of brown shoes in sight! You would see them on people walking down the street, on display in store windows, on people getting out of their cars; you'd be noticing them everywhere."

"Yes, I'm sure you're right," I responded.

"But on the other hand," he continued, " if I didn't tell you ahead of time that I was going to pay you a hundred dollars for each pair, we would have spent the entire day together and you wouldn't have even noticed a single pair, would you? But because the financial gain component came into play, brown shoes became important to you; they were worth a hundred dollars a pair! But if I hadn't offered that, you would've been oblivious to them."

"That's interesting, Zors, but what's your point?" I asked, still stumped.

"What's my point? Don't you see this as a key to getting what you want from life?" he said.

"I'm sorry, Zors, but I have no idea what you're talking about," I said defeatedly.

Zors revealed amazing patience as he continued. "Okay, let's talk about information. There's a ton of it out there and you're being barraged by it every single day. You're exposed to so much, in fact, that your conscious mind can't handle it all. Fortunately, the conscious mind has a filter, or tuner, to reduce its exposure to only the information that's important to it. Without it, the conscious mind would not be able to focus effectively on any of its tasks."

"How come I'm not aware of the additional information that's being screened out?" I asked. "If it's being filtered, or tuned out, I guess the filter must be working. So where is this filter anyway?"

"The filter, or tuner, is your subconscious mind," Zors shared. "Once your conscious mind effectively tells your subconscious what's important, it tunes your internal receiver into that information. It blocks out all the rest, much like a radio that's tuned in to a favorite station.

"If we were all sitting in a restaurant right now," he went on, "we could *physically* hear the chatter but not the details, of people talking around us, unless they were loud enough to be intrusive. However, we wouldn't hear them *consciously*. Why? Because we'd be concentrating on our own conversation. However, even if the people sitting at the table next to us were speaking softly, and mentioned your name only once as part of their conversation, you'd hear it. Your internal receiver knows your name is important, so you are always consciously tuned in to hear it.

"The same is true in our brown shoes example. You didn't consciously see brown shoes until your subconscious knew they were important, and then you saw them everywhere.

"Let's say your rich uncle died and left you a hundred thousand dollars. You decide to invest it, but know nothing about investing. It has never been important to you because you never had any money to invest. Now suddenly it is important to you, so you begin a process of researching methods by which to invest.

"During the time you're actively searching the web for what you need, you begin noticing that you're stumbling over investment information in your everyday life. What a coincidence! You start hearing stock reports on the radio which never registered with you before. You even begin hearing people on the elevator talking about investing, which is something you never noticed in the past.

"The point of all this isn't that you were all of a sudden, by some strange accident, exposed to a lot of information on investing. You've *always* been exposed to this information. It's just that it had never been that important to you before, so you simply didn't have the need to notice it—you weren't tuned in to it! So think of all the information out there that you don't realize is important—life-changing information about your health, financial well-being, spirituality, or whatever. It's all out there, and once you become aware of it and learn how to tune in to and apply it, you can accomplish almost anything."

"Wow!" I exclaimed, "This is pretty deep stuff. So how do I tune in to all this great information?"

"That," he said, "we'll save for another night. It's time for us to go now."

I was so excited to learn more I just couldn't believe Zors was going to take off without answering my question. What was the information that was out there and how do I get it? He had me totally mesmerized, and was going to make me wait before he'd share the secret! I desperately wanted him to share it right then and there.

"Surely you can stay for a few minutes longer," I pleaded. "Maybe have another cup of coffee?"

"No, no," he replied, "I have to get up early in the morning. Thanks for the wonderful evening." Then, as quick as that, he and Ruth were gone.

It was as if Zors had played a clever trick on me. For the next few days, I racked my brain trying to imagine what information could be out there that would change my life, and how I could possibly get access to it. It really ate at me because I knew what he said made sense. Deep down inside, I'd had a gnawing feeling of dissatisfaction for quite some time, but had just been ignoring it—thinking there was nothing I could do about it. All my friends seemed to be doing things the same way I was, and I thought this must be all there was to life. But now I was beginning to get a glimmer of hope....

"Zors doesn't share this information with everyone. He wants to be certain you need to know it; otherwise you probably aren't five-percent material. Zors throws out seeds all the time to people, but few pick up on them. He has to know you will value the information when you get it, use it with integrity and share it with others. He didn't give you the whole story on purpose; he's waiting for you to ask him everything you asked me."

—Mark Webster

—Chapter 5—

The Inside Story

"Hello, Mark, this is Jonathan. What's out there?"
I asked.
"What do you mean?" he replied.

Mark Webster had been associated in business with Zors for six years, which had obviously been quite good for him. He was very happy as a leader in Zors' organization, and it was clear he was making a great deal of money. He seemed to be blossoming under Zors' tutelage and thought the world of him. I had a feeling Mark would know what Zors was referring to when he told me about my needing to capture certain information, so I gave him a call.

"I'm talking about some earth-shattering information that is 'out there,'" I continued. "I haven't a clue what Zors is talking about and he wouldn't tell me."

Mark laughed. "So he told you about the internal receiver, did he? So what do you think?"

"I thought it was interesting, but he left out the ending. WHAT'S OUT THERE?" I shouted at a surprised Mark. I normally didn't shout but I was getting exasperated.

"Well, to start with, Zors is testing you," Mark said.

"Testing me for what?" I asked, my patience wearing thin. I couldn't seem to get Mark to say anything of any consequence on the subject.

"To see if you are in the five percent or the ninety-five percent," he answered.

"Mark, now you're really getting on my nerves. You and Zors are talking to me in a foreign language, probably as some kind of inside joke."

"He does have a great sense of humor, doesn't he?" Mark chuckled.

"Then it *is* a joke," I replied.

"Alright, let me tell you a little more about Michael Zors; maybe this'll help," he said. "He functions on a completely different level from anyone you've ever known. He could share knowledge with you that would give you the tools to accomplish anything you want in life. He's very selective in terms of who he chooses to associate with because he doesn't like to waste his time. He needs to be sure you definitely want and will apply this special information."

"It seems like you might be exaggerating a little bit Mark," I said. "He's functioning on a different level, yet he can help me accomplish anything I want in my life? Just a little over the top, don't you think?"

"Jonathan, listen carefully." Mark continued, "When I started working with Zors, I was living paycheck to paycheck. I weighed 222 pounds and played golf like a small child. In those six years, I have increased my net worth by seven figures, lost 38 pounds, and have a six handicap on the golf course. All of this was possible because I listened to Zors and applied what he taught me."

"You would be a millionaire if you increased your net worth by seven figures," I scoffed. "I think you meant six figures."

"Seven figures," he replied.

There was a moment of silence as I digested all of this.

"Alright, now you're starting to get me excited. Tell me what's 'out there' and explain that five-percent comment."

"The five percent refers to the group who makes things happen. Zors believes that five percent of the people run the world, while the other ninety-five go along for the ride."

"Sure," I said, "the five percent that have all the money."

"Well, it's true that most of them are wealthy, and there's a very good reason for that. But wealth isn't the common denominator. The five percenters are the leaders; they get things done. They take on the responsibility of causing positive change and then make it happen!"

"Okay, that makes some sense, but WHAT'S OUT THERE?" I asked.

"I'm going to defer to Zors on that one. I'll let him explain it to you."

"Oh, come on," I begged. "I have no idea when I'll get to see him again. Please, just tell me."

Mark's voice lowered to a more confidential level. "First of all, Zors has a very unique method of teaching. It's as if he causes you to discover the information within yourself. Secondly, all you have to do is go next door and ask him."

"I can't think of an excuse to go see him," I whined.

"You really aren't getting any of this, are you?" Mark responded. "Zors doesn't share this information with everyone. He wants to be certain you need to know it; otherwise you probably aren't five-percent material. Zors throws out seeds all the time to people, but few pick up on them. He has to know you will value the information when you get it and use it with integrity and share it with others. He didn't give you the whole story on purpose; he's waiting for you to ask him everything you asked me. Once again, he and Ruth are the smartest, kindest, most caring people I know. As far as Zors goes, you need to get to know him and his philosophy. Go next door, Jonathan, and talk to him. He's always looking to help others."

" **A**nyone who's under the influence of an internal locus of control believes he or she can get from point A to point B, no matter what. They find a way to make this happen in spite of any hurdles. Nothing or no one can stop the successful completion of the task."

—Zors

—Chapter 6—

What's a Locus of Control?

Two days went by before I got up enough courage to go over to see Zors. Actually there had been a lot of visitors to his house during that time, and I didn't want to interrupt him. Well, to be truthful, maybe I was just using that as an excuse. I finally knocked on the door at seven o'clock on a Sunday night.

When the door opened, Ruth was standing there smiling at me and said, "Jonathan, good to see you. I suppose you're here to see Zors."

It took me a few seconds to respond. I was surprised that she, too, called him Zors and already knew I was there to see him.

"Yes, is he busy? I don't want to disturb him."

"Oh, he's just packing for our trip. We're going to Florida for two weeks, you know. I'll get him. He's been expecting you."

Why had he been expecting me? I didn't get much of a chance to think about that as he was there in an instant.

"Hi, Jonathan," he said. "Have a seat. Would you like something to drink? Ruth just made some iced tea."

I just shook my head and blurted out, "What's out there?"

"I don't think anything," he responded. "Earlier I saw some squirrels and a few birds, but I don't think there's much out there now."

"That's not what I am talking about," I stammered. When I looked in his eyes I saw an impish gleam and realized he knew *exactly* what I meant.

"You hinted about information that exists outside my frame of reference, which can open up a whole new world to me. I'm extremely interested in tuning in to this information," I explained.

"Why?" he asked. "What would you use it for at this point in your life?"

Why won't he just tell me? Is he playing some kind of mind game with me? I better just answer him and hope for the best, I thought to myself.

"I'm sure I can use this information for many situations. Right now, for example, I'm pretty frustrated at work."

"Oh, what's the problem?" Zors asked.

"Well, my boss is constantly getting on my nerves. He could do a lot more to help me complete some of my projects, but he's not at all supportive. He's making my life miserable."

Zors seemed very interested. "So maybe if you had a more supportive boss, your entire life would be better."

"That's probably true," I agreed.

"So, is your boss in control of your happiness?"

That certainly didn't sound right. "Well, no," I said haltingly. "I just meant that...."

"Hold on, son," Zors interrupted. "Are you familiar with the term *locus of control*?"

"Not really."

"Well, then let's talk about it."

Suddenly, I felt very different than when I walked in. The mood had changed abruptly. A feeling of peaceful comfort came over me as if I were about to hear my dad tell me a caring story. I don't know how Zors had engineered it, but our relationship had changed—right then and there. I was no longer intimidated; he was now my friend.

Zors began speaking quietly, "Studies have been done as to what makes people happy and what doesn't. I can explain this best by using alpha dogs as an example. Do you know anything about alpha dogs?"

"A little," I responded. "Dogs are pack animals and one of the dogs in the pack is the leader. That's the alpha dog."

"Good, anything else?"

"That's all I know," I said.

"Well, I had a pet alpha dog that used to meow all the time. I found out he was taking a foreign language!"

"What?" I said.

"It's a joke, Jonathan. Lighten up. Anyway, say the alpha dog's a male. He knows he's the alpha dog and takes his job seriously—very seriously. He's responsible for all the other dogs in the pack."

"Is this leading anywhere Zors?" I asked, "Or are you setting me up for another joke?"

"No, this is serious stuff. Now listen. When you own one dog, he often believes he is in charge of the 'pack'—the pack being you and your family. There are ways to teach the dog he's not in charge but, if you don't, he thinks he's the alpha dog. This, of course, can cause major problems. One of the biggest is when you and your family aren't home. In his mind, he's supposed to be in control of the pack, but there's no one at home to control or take care of. Since he can't do his job, he becomes frustrated. He's not in control of the situation, so he lets everyone know of his displeasure. He chews up the furniture or relieves himself in the house, or whatever, to send this message.

"Now, how does this relate to the human world? Humans who believe they are in control of their lives are happier than those who believe others are in control. Like the alpha dog, not having control leads to a feeling of frustration and unhappiness. Believing you are the captain of your own ship is defined as an internal locus of control, as opposed to an external locus of control."

"Well, I'm in control of my life," I argued, "but others have an influence."

"The statement you just made reveals that you're still under the influence of an external locus of control. Let me explain.

"Anyone who's under the influence of an internal locus of control believes he can get from point A to point B, no matter what. He finds a way to make this happen in spite of any hurdles. Nothing or no one can stop the successful completion of the task.

"One who is under the influence of an external locus of control believes others affect the outcome. He believes he can complete the task only if everyone else is on board. He always has an underlying feeling of tension because he believes others can change the outcome. Like the owners of the alpha dog who's alone at home, he believes he has little, if any, influence on the outcome."

Just then, I heard the doorbell ring and Ruth went to answer it. Zors ignored it and kept talking.

"For instance, take me," he continued. "Very early in life, I functioned as if I were a victim. I thought everyone else was responsible for my miserable life and I was just stuck. I was miserable and, because like attracts like, I attracted misery and other miserable people into my life.

"One day I decided I just couldn't take it anymore. I made the decision that I was done being a victim. I decided to become the hero of my own life. I started accepting responsibility for everything bad that ever happened to me, and decided to feel good about all future victories."

"How did you flip the switch just like that?" I asked. "If I believe I'm under the influence of an external locus of control, I can't just *will* it to be an internal one."

Just then, Ruth came into the room and told Zors he had a guest in the library.

"Yes, Ron said he was coming. Please tell him I'll be right there."

"Jonathan, please excuse me. I really need to meet with this fellow. I'm going to be gone for two weeks and I need to review some things with him before I leave.

"But, quickly, to answer your question, once you learn how to capture and use the powerful information that's out there, you'll know you can accomplish anything you set your mind to and take action on. At that point, you will have elected to be under the influence of an internal locus of control."

"That's probably true, but how can I get anyone to steer me to this information?" I asked.

"I promise I will explain all that to you when I get back from Florida," he replied. "I'm sorry, but I really have to meet with Ron now."

"What if I could wave a magic wand and make all your old bad habits go away, while injecting you with a whole new set of good habits? Can you imagine the impact that would have on your life?"

—Zors

—Chapter 7—

The Magic Wand

Having to wait two whole weeks to talk to Zors seemed like an eternity. I did a lot of soul searching about my locus of control and had to admit that I believed my life was under the control of others. I despised the thought. I really wanted more control, but didn't know how to go about getting it. I was anxious for Zors to return.

Halfway through the second week, I got a surprise telephone call; it was Zors!

"Jonathan," he said, "I'll be back next week and thought maybe we could meet for an early breakfast next Tuesday. If you want to come over at about six-thirty, we'll have a little breakfast and we can talk."

"I'll be there. Thanks!"

"See you then," he replied.

Obviously, I was very excited. Finally, I was going to get an answer to my question. I was thankful he had called me, but I really didn't think he'd remember his promise. Who am I to him anyway? After all, Zors had important business to take care of. Why would he want to waste his time with me?

Years later, I would understand what a promise meant to Zors. At the time, however, it just made me feel good to have him remember me.

Zors arrived home Sunday night and I had to force myself to resist the urge to run over and pick his brain. He had just returned from his trip, and I was sure he wasn't interested in being bothered. I told myself that Tuesday would get here fast enough. Even so, I couldn't help but wonder if I was expecting too much. Could there really be a nugget of information I could use to turn my life around?

When I walked over to Zors' house Tuesday morning, he was at the door waiting for me.

"How are you?" I asked.

"Well, I could have woke up grumpy this morning, but I let her sleep in!" he quipped, smilingly broadly. "Come on in and have some breakfast with me."

Sitting on the table was an enormous spread; pancakes, bacon, eggs, juice, and coffee—enough to feed an army.

"Is anyone else coming?" I asked, looking around.

"No, just us. I always have a big breakfast because I don't eat much the rest of the day. But I'm sure you're not here to talk about food."

"No, not really. I'm anxious to find out what you're going to give me in the way of information that will change my life."

"Well, to be perfectly honest," he replied, "I'm not going to give you information that will change your life. I don't know enough about you to do that."

"Then what are we talking about here?" was my frustrated reply.

"I'll share a technique with you that will assist you in capturing the specific information you need to accomplish your goals. I'm sure the information you need is different than what I or anyone else might need. Your life, after all, is unique, but the technique has universal application in helping anyone achieve greater success."

I got so confused, I didn't know what to ask next. Fortunately, he continued. "First of all, you need to understand the nature of knowledge. Let me tell you a story. Many years ago I was the youngest salesman at the company where I used to work. We were required to attend an all-day productivity-enhancing seminar at a local college. There were about thirty of us, but everyone else was ten to thirty years older than me."

"All of them were special. No one made a lot of money, even though each one had a unique way of serving others. The company just attracted those kinds of people, although they certainly weren't great examples of successful sales executives.

"That seminar was fantastic, as I was exposed to many techniques on improving productivity. I took a ton of notes, barely keeping up with the speaker.

"The next morning, I began asking the others their opinions of the program. I told them I was impressed and excited, but every single one of them responded in the same negative way. 'The seminar was boring,' they complained. 'All that information is just the same old stuff we all learned years ago,' they concluded.

"I was stunned. I thought the information was valid and dynamic. If they all knew all that stuff, then *why weren't they more successful?* That's when the light went on. *It's not enough to just know a dynamic technique; you need to use it on a regular basis to get better results.*"

"So knowing isn't enough?" I asked.

"Once again, let's take the game of golf," Zors replied. "I can read a book on how to swing a club correctly, but that doesn't mean I'm going to be able to do it. The fact that I know how to do it, doesn't mean I automatically can do it. I need to apply that knowledge to reconstruct my swing piece by piece. I need to take each aspect of the swing and practice it until it becomes second nature to me, before I go on to the next aspect. Once I'm able to put all the correct aspects together, my game will improve. If, as I'm playing, I have to actively think about all those aspects, I'm unlikely to improve my game. I need to be in the *habit* of swinging more correctly and effectively. But this can happen only when I use the knowledge and make it a part of my experience."

I finally understood. "I need to use the knowledge I obtain by making it part of who I am and what I do," I offered.

"Exactly," Zors agreed. "Successful people are in the habit of doing things that once seemed impossible for them to do, whereas unsuccessful people think they can't or simply won't. But there's more. Once you start the process of changing your habit patterns and improving various areas of your life, you'll become aware of even more of the wonderful information that's out there to help you be more successful—sort of like the brown shoes."

"I see," I said. "I need to take one piece of positive new information, learn what to do with it, and consciously do it over and over again until it becomes a habit. After that, I move on to the next piece."

"You understand the concept," he said. "What you are suggesting will work, but it's rather slow and tedious. Using that method could take you a long time to get yourself to where you want to be."

"Great," I replied. "Then I guess I'm back to square one."

"No, not really," Zors encouraged. "You're definitely on the right track. It's just that there's a faster and more effective way to get there. All you really need to do is reprogram your mind."

"What does that mean?" I asked.

"Well, you've been programming your mind all these years as you've lived your life. You've developed a lot of habit patterns which you don't even think about. Some of those subconscious habits serve you very well; others not so well or not at all. What if I could wave a magic wand and make all your old bad habits go away, while injecting you with a whole new set of good habits? Can you imagine the impact that would have on your life?"

"I sure can. Where do you keep this magic wand?"

Zors was smiling broadly. "Do you know how important even one idea can be?" he asked. "For example, if it weren't for one idea Edison had, we'd all be reading by gas or candlelight. The magic wand is an idea; a concept that can quickly and permanently change the course of your life."

Now, I was getting very excited. Zors had a quick and easy way to turn me into a success. I couldn't wait to hear what was coming next.

Zors continued, "I'll bet you think this idea is a quick and easy way to make your life better, don't you?"

"That's exactly what I was thinking," I answered. "I guess, by the way you asked, I'm wrong."

"No, you're absolutely right!" he exclaimed. "This magic wand will definitely work; all you need to do is use it correctly and consistently. But for some strange reason, which is beyond me, only about five percent of the population uses it. While many are exposed to it, only a few take advantage of it, and I'll never understand why. This is sad not only for them, but also for those they say they love."

"I'll use it, I promise!" I said, sounding like a small child.

"Well, here's the deal," he continued. "If I share this idea with you, you have to promise to use it for thirty days. If, after thirty days, you don't start experiencing a major change in your life, you can stop and forget about it. If it works, however, you have to stick with it, use it consistently for the rest of your life, and share it with others."

"I totally agree to that," I blurted out. "What is it?"

"If I'm going to share this with you, and do it justice, I need more time. I really have to make some calls now, but if you want to meet Saturday morning, we can go through the process in detail," Zors assured.

It was a letdown not to get the information immediately, but Saturday wasn't the end of the world. I was beginning to think Zors would delay these meetings on purpose to get me more excited about them. I was like a kid before Christmas looking forward to what Santa would bring. Christmas day was great, but the anticipation leading up to it was even more exciting.

"Okay," I agreed, "why don't you come over to my house for breakfast?"

"Thank you," he replied, "but I have an early breakfast appointment downtown that day. Why don't you meet me here at the house around nine o'clock and we'll talk in my office? I should be back by then."

"I'll be there."

"The magic wand is an idea; a concept that can quickly and permanently change the course of your life. It will definitely work; all you need to do is use it correctly and consistently. While many are exposed to it, only a few take advantage of it, and I'll never understand why. This is sad not only for them, but also for those they say they love."

—Zors

"The beliefs held in your subconscious affect your life immeasurably. It's your best friend and more. It is your obedient servant and will always cause you to act on whatever beliefs you program into it. Most of your life is lived based on what your subconscious is led to believe. It dictates whether you fail or succeed, have a poor lifestyle or a great one."

—Zors

—Chapter 8—

The Process and How It Works

By the time Saturday rolled around, the excitement had almost disappeared. I pessimistically had the sinking feeling that I was never really going to learn any life-changing technique. What could possibly be so effective?

Zors had already taught me some interesting concepts, but nothing earth-shattering. I suppose I could start forming better habits, but Zors was right about how slow that process was. Even so, it was probably better than just standing still. Well, it wouldn't be long before I knew how important this meeting would be.

As I walked up to the door, Zors was just pulling in from his mysterious breakfast appointment in town. We walked in together.

His office projected a somewhat different image of Zors than the rest of the house. It was immense, with an obviously expensive mahogany desk and credenza. A burgundy-colored leather couch was against the far wall, while two matching overstuffed chairs flanked a coordinating mahogany coffee table. On it was a finely crafted model of a business jet named *Freedom*, which he could view from behind his desk. There was a large mahogany conference table with six chairs near the other wall. The artwork was all of an aeronautical nature, appeared to be original, and was tastefully arranged.

"Nice office," I said. "I didn't know you were into flying."

"Yes," he replied. "My mentor taught me that it's important to reflect success while surrounding yourself with things you enjoy. It has a positive, uplifting effect on me and seems to inspire others as well as increase my credibility."

I suddenly began to realize that there was a purpose to everything this man did. He was careful to downplay his accomplishments, humbly giving credit to his mentor. His business, which Mark had said was international in scope, was obviously a highly successful enterprise.

As soon as we sat down, I on the couch and he on one of the large chairs, Zors began, "I know you've been frustrated by getting only bits and pieces of this process I've alluded to, so let's get down to business. I will now share a methodology with you that is so effective that it can forever change your life in a positive way. It's a method which will enable you to change your habit patterns."

Zors continued, "I'm sure you've heard that we humans use only five to ten percent of our brains. But let's give ourselves the benefit of the doubt and assume it's ten. If so, we only need to use twenty percent of our brains to double our mental productivity. Now think about this for a minute: If we're using only twenty percent of our potential, we're wasting eighty, right? Can you think of any other resource where we're wasting eighty percent? That would be almost criminal, yet this is how poorly we're utilizing our minds. And remember, that eighty percent waste is only after we've doubled our output, otherwise it's ninety."

"Well, then I'm probably wasting ninety-eight percent," I laughed.

"Not really, Jonathan," Zors said in a serious tone. "The point I'm making is that doubling your mental output isn't that great a task because you'll be using only twenty percent of your potential. If you double your mental output, you could at least double your productivity. Just think how successful you would be if you doubled your contribution to the world."

"Wow, that's pretty powerful stuff!" I said. "But how many years will it take for me to learn how to expand my mind like that?"

"One-twelfth," he answered.

"What?"

"One-twelfth of a year; about a month."

I got that feeling again. "You're not going to tell me that you will teach me this a month from now, are you?"

"No, when you leave here today, you can continue the process in the correct way."

"Continue *what* process? I'm not in the process of anything."

"Ah, but you are," Zors was really getting focused now. "All your life you've been programming your subconscious mind. Some of what you programmed was good; some was not so good. This is reflected in the results you've been getting in your personal and professional life. Now you can use a process you have been using your whole life to reprogram yourself in areas where you'd like to get better results. You can get rid of bad programming and inject as much good programming as you wish. This process will have a major impact on a lot of aspects of your life, one being the development of more positive habits."

"So I can get rid of my bad habits and create good ones, and do it all in just one month?"

When he responded with an affirmative nod, I continued with a concern. "I'm not sure I know what my bad habits are.

As a matter of fact, I'm really not too sure about the good ones either."

"It doesn't matter," he said. "Let me explain the process and how it affects the brain, and then you'll have a better understanding."

"Okay," I said breathlessly. He had me all excited again.

"Your brain is extremely powerful; more powerful than any computer on earth. Think about having the most expensive, most advanced computer there is, and using it only as a word processor. That's how most people use their minds. But with a little training, you can expand your mind-computer from a word processor to a fully utilized giant IBM mainframe.

"Now let's talk about two aspects of your mind: the conscious and the subconscious. They both have certain responsibilities, but they also work together. We'll talk about the third aspect, the creative subconscious, later.

"Your conscious mind enables you to knowingly do things. But it can also be used to reach the subconscious, which it has been doing all your life.

"Your conscious mind receives information and you either act on it or you don't. It also presents that information to the subconscious, which either accepts it or rejects it. If the subconscious accepts the information, it has started believing in it. Whether the information is true or not doesn't matter; it's whatever the subconscious can be led to *believe*!

"Your subconscious is very stubborn; it has to be convinced before it'll accept something new or different. There are basically three components necessary to do that: (1) give it information with strong emotion; (2) give it information from a credible source, like a loving parent or mentor; and (3) give it information over and over again.

"After a loving parent has continually and enthusiastically told his or her child that he or she is smart, the child's subconscious begins believing it. The message is conveyed often, by a credible source, with emotion. This bolsters the child's self-esteem, which can be hurt or enhanced, especially by parents or others the child respects.

"The beliefs held in your subconscious affect your life immeasurably. It's simply impossible to overstate how important it is. It is your best friend and more. It is your obedient servant and will always cause you to act on whatever beliefs are programmed into it. Most of your life is lived based on what your subconscious is led to believe."

"What do you mean?" I asked.

"Well, think about some firsts in your life. Do you remember the first time you tried to drive a car? You had to consciously think about each aspect of driving, such as when to step on the gas or brake and when to shift. At first, it was difficult to think of all those things at once; you had to think hard to drive. Now, however, you drive without having to think about all the rudimentary aspects. You can be talking to someone, listening to the radio, deep in thought about your life, or whatever, while automatically keeping a keen eye out for avoiding potential challenges. You aren't thinking about basic driving skills. You've programmed your subconscious on what to do and when to do it, so now you drive under the influence of your subconscious.

"What about the first time you drove to where you work? Chances are you had to learn where your place of work was and the best route you could take to get there. You probably looked at a map or went on the computer to plan your trip and then consciously followed your planned route. Now you drive to work automatically, subconsciously. I'll bet there were days you've gone to work when you didn't even remember how you got there!"

"Yes, that happens to me sometimes—especially when I'm really 'zoned out.'"

"Well, that's because your subconscious is directing you to go where you programmed it to send you."

"But can't your conscious mind override your subconscious?" As soon as I asked that question, I knew I was being stupid, but Zors was careful not to hurt my feelings.

"First of all, you need to remember that much of what you do is already programmed into your subconscious. There's too much going on for the conscious mind to override it all. Your subconscious mind is one of the most powerful forces on earth!"

"Zors," I interrupted, "aren't you getting a little carried away?"

I think Zors was perturbed by my comment. And after thinking about it for a moment, I began to understand what he was saying.

"Okay, I apologize for that question. Obviously, you're serious. I get it that the subconscious is not something to be ignored."

Zors' mood changed abruptly again. It was like someone had thrown a switch. He smiled and continued in a gentle, thoughtful manner. "You're right Jonathan. Your subconscious mind is the director of your life. It controls the tuner of your internal receiver and all your habit patterns. Your subconscious also contains the beliefs and information that drive you to do what you do. All your beliefs, whether they are failure- or success-inducing, are stored there. It dictates your habits and lifestyle—how you conduct yourself and live."

"So, if I change my belief system, my way of life changes?" I asked.

"Yes, everything is created inside, before it manifests outside. Take the couch you're sitting on. Before it came to be, someone had to imagine it in his mind. Once he had a mental picture of it, he drew it. The couch was then built using his drawing as a guide. Nothing exists on the outside which isn't first created on the inside.

"Now, let's take this a step further. Let's say that when you were in first grade, you brought home an arithmetic test paper from school. You got an 'F' because you had not yet caught on to that early level of mathematics. When your mother saw that paper, she mistakenly said, 'Too bad, you're just not very good in arithmetic.' Your father compounded the problem by saying, 'He's no mathematician.'

"Every time you did poorly in math after that, your parents affirmed that you weren't good in math. Since these comments were hurtful and embarrassing to you, you attached a lot of emotion to them. Your subconscious kept getting an emotional message which told it you were no good in math. Guess what? Your subconscious sees to it that you're bad in math because it believes that is the way it is. It believes that is what you want and serves you without question."

"How does it make sure I'm bad in math?" I asked.

"First of all, it blocks information about math that you could be absorbing. Your internal receiver is not tuned in to math. Then it disturbs your focus when working on math problems by allowing other thoughts to go through your mind—thoughts it believes are more important to you. It's simply being the dutiful servant that it is, serving you well by ensuring that you aren't good in math."

"Wait a minute," I said. "When I first met you, I told you I had a bad sense of direction. I remember you telling me that was an affirmation that would serve me well. Were you referring to programming my subconscious mind in a negative way?"

Zors looked at me with a touch of admiration. "You're quite smart, aren't you? And you're exactly right. It's not just your parents who program you; it can be anyone you believe, especially yourself!"

"I can program myself?" I asked in disbelief.

"That's the point of this whole conversation," he said. "More than anyone else, you program yourself. You do it every day; you've done it all your life. Now you need to do it knowingly, with a purpose."

"With a purpose," I reiterated.

"Yes, by design. By taking a systematic approach to reprogramming your subconscious, you can tell it what you want it to believe and what you want it to discard. You can do this by using affirmations."

"You mean like verbally pronouncing something is true?"

"Here's what I mean," he said. "Let's take your so-called sense of direction challenge. First of all, never refer to it as a 'direction challenge.' Never say anything negative about your ability to get where you are going. Your self-talk is key.

"Create an affirmation—a single, positive, first person, 'I,' present-tense statement of the truth in advance. It can be something like: *I have a great sense of direction, and I always know where I'm going.* Start saying that to yourself twice a day; once in the morning and once in the evening. And say it with as much emotion as you can muster."

"How do I get emotional about having a good sense of direction?" I asked.

"Use your imagination. Were you ever in a situation where it was important for you to be somewhere at a certain time, and you got lost? You started feeling anxious, but then after some trial and error, you suddenly found the place you were searching for."

"That has happened a few times," I admitted.

"Well, do you recall the feeling of relief you had when you realized you were there on time?"

"I sure do."

"So, recapture that feeling—that emotion—and project it into your affirmation. As you affirm your wonderful sense of direction, accompany it with that positive emotion."

"I think the negative emotion of the fear of not getting there on time would work better for me," I surmised.

"That may sound like a great idea, but it's totally wrong," he stated. "Do you know anything about the left and right brain?"

"I know about right and wrong brain. Mine is normally wrong," thinking that was quite funny.

"Is that another one of your great affirmations that will serve you well?" he asked.

"Zors, I'm only kidding."

"Yes, but your self-talk, kidding or not, is creating who you are becoming. You need to watch your self-talk."

"Okay!"

Zors continued, "Now there are two spheres of your brain: left and right. Your left brain is the logical side, you know 'L' for logical, and your right brain is the creative side. Without going into a long dissertation, the right brain thinks in pictures. If you tell a right-brained dominant kid not to slam the door, he or she sees a picture of a door slamming—and keeps slamming the door. It is more effective to say that the door needs to be closed quietly. Parents get frustrated because they don't understand why they can't get their kids to do what they're told. Often, it's because they're using negative pictures when they tell their kids what to do. But the mind can't focus on the opposite of an idea!"

"Now you tell me! I hope it's not too late for my kids." I was still trying to be funny, but Zors was looking at me like what I said definitely wasn't a joke. He was quite serious.

"When you use these affirmations you are affecting the right brain," he continued. "Project positive pictures so you can create positive results. Negative pictures create only negative results."

"You made your point Zors. I can take any change I want to make in myself, affirm it twice a day with positive emotion, and eventually the change will actually take place."

"Absolutely," he replied.

"It sounds too easy, but I'll give it a try. How long does it take for the change to take place?"

"Don't worry about that now. There's a lot more to this than I've told you. You need to make some discoveries about this process before we continue any further. For the time being, work with the affirmation about your great sense of direction. Say the affirmation religiously, twice a day for the next two weeks, and then we can meet again and take it from there."

"One more thing. Don't give it a try. Do it! Trying doesn't work. Trying is a cop out. You either do something or you don't. Let me give you an example," Zors continued as he picked up a pen and held it in the palm of his hand. "Try to pick up this pen," he said.

I went to reach for it and hesitated. "Oh my gosh," I said to Zors. "I understand. I can't try to pick it up. I either pick it up or I don't!"

"You've got it Jonathan. You're a winner. Ninety-five percenters don't get it about try, but you did! Congratulations."

"Thanks, Zors, I needed that. So why don't I do four or five affirmations? I want to grow as quickly as possible. I mean if one affirmation is good, more should be better, right?"

"For now just do the one," he said, "then let's meet here at my office at the same time two weeks from today."

I agreed to do it Zors' way, although I was anxious to change many more habits than one. I didn't know that, while the habit-changing piece was important, the process had much more to offer than just that. The truly amazing part was yet to come.

"I *agreed to do it Zors' way, although I was anxious to change many more habits than one. I didn't know that, while the habit-changing piece was important, the process had much more to offer than just that. The truly amazing part was yet to come."*

—Jonathan Weatherby

"**I**f you knew for a fact that you could achieve any goal you desired, wouldn't you set even greater goals?"

—Zors

—Chapter 9—

The Creative Subconscious

"It's been a fascinating two weeks," I told Zors at our next meeting. "Something weird is starting to happen to me."

"Does it have anything to do with your internal receiver?" he asked with a twinkle in his eye.

"It sure does," I answered. "It's a little eerie!"

"Tell me about it, Jonathan." Zors knew where I was going with this, but he encouraged me to share it anyway.

"Well, first of all, I wanted to make sure I was reprogramming enough, so I repeated my affirmations four times a day: driving to work, at lunch, driving home, and at bedtime."

"Twice a day is enough," Zors said, "but the more often you affirm, the faster it happens."

"Something strange started happening though, after five or six days. I'm always lost in thought when I drive to work, and I let my subconscious, as you say, concern itself about getting me there. Recently, I started realizing that I was beginning to notice landmarks. I was also noticing street names and even discovered another way to go. I'm now supersensitive to the geographical layout of the city. It's like I'm looking at this town through someone else's eyes."

"That's your internal receiver's tuner supporting you in being a person with a great sense of direction."

"Wow, that's what I suspected. But it's *so* different from how I've functioned for years that it's almost scary."

"Great," Zors said with a smile. "This is exactly what I wanted you to experience. When people get into this program full speed ahead, they are often surprised by the information that comes pouring in. It's easy to believe that the sudden access to all this pertinent information is just a coincidence, but it isn't. It's the internal receiver's tuner doing exactly what it's supposed to do. Expect this to continue to happen in response to your affirmations; that way you won't get totally freaked out."

"Will do, Zors. Notice I didn't say try!"

"Good, now we can plug into the really magical part of this whole process."

I was very anxious to hear what he had to say next, but I had a burning question to ask first.

"Zors, why are you doing all this?"

"All what?"

"Spending all this time and sharing all this information with me. I know how busy you are and how valuable your time is. Why me?"

"Well, you're my neighbor," he said warmly.

"That's true," I said, "but you have a lot of neighbors and we've only just gotten to know each other."

Zors looked at me pensively for what seemed to be an eternity. Finally he spoke.

"Jonathan, you're right; there's another reason. I really would prefer not to share that with you today, but I promise I will in the future.

It was such a strange response that I honestly didn't know what to say, so I paused for a moment. "Fine. Whenever you feel the time's right."

"Alright, back to business," he continued. "Let me tell you what affirmations are great at doing—causing stress!"

"Hey, Zors," I interrupted, "I've got plenty of stress already, like most people do. Just look at these fingernails!"

"That's probably because you have the wrong kind of stress, Jonathan. I'm talking about *constructive* stress—the kind that can help you create significant rewards for yourself. Let me start with a question. Tell me, how do you establish goals and then go about reaching them?"

"Well, let me see," I replied. "I guess my first step is to determine what I want or need, then evaluate the possibility of obtaining it. Once I'm convinced it's reachable, I set several intermediate goals. Then I find a way to achieve each intermediate goal until I reach the final goal."

"That seems like a pretty standard approach," Zors said. "Has it worked well for you in the past?"

"I think so," I said proudly. "I've been able to achieve most of my goals."

Then Zors asked the zinger. "Then you are completely satisfied with your life, to this point in time?"

"Well, like everyone else, I'm satisfied with some parts and not satisfied with others."

Zors began grilling me. "Well, let me rephrase the question: Are you where you want to be in life?"

"Well, no, not really. I've been working for the same company for several years now and haven't gotten a raise in two years, which hasn't helped my debt load any. The longer I stay, the more they seem to own me. I feel like a puppet on a string who's really not going anywhere."

"How about physically? Are you as fit as you would like?"

"I suppose I could lose some weight and tone up a bit. I just haven't had the time...."

Zors interrupted, "How your about education? Are you where you need to be?"

"Getting there," I responded, now dubious of exactly how well I was doing. "I went to college but that isn't earning me the big money I thought it would. I even did some graduate work, but it didn't seem to matter."

"Well, Jonathan, what part of your life *is* where it needs to be?"

"I have a nice family," I replied, "a great wife and two terrific kids."

"Are the kids all set for college? I mean, do you have the funds established for their education? Do you have sufficient insurance to care for your family if you die prematurely or can't work? Do you have an emergency fund established in case of an unexpected financial setback? What about retirement savings?"

"Wow, I don't have all of that, but I have a wonderful family. Each one of them knows she's loved."

"I believe that, John, and that's great," Zors said, "but that's not my point. I'm just endeavoring to show you that your method of attaining goals may not have served you as well as you might have thought."

"I disagree," I said defensively. "My way works just fine. I've already accomplished significant goals in my life. To get where you're talking about, at this point, would be practically impossible."

"So you're saying no one your age has ever reached the level I've described?"

"Well, maybe, but that really has nothing to do with my ability to set and reach goals."

Zors was quiet for what seemed like an eternity. When he finally spoke, his voice was soft and calm, "Jonathan, what if you knew for a fact that you could achieve *any* goal you desired, wouldn't you have set even greater goals?"

"That's not a valid question, and you know it. No one can reach any goal he desires."

Zors smiled and exclaimed, "Now that's an affirmation that will serve you well!"

"Come on, Zors," I said, exasperated. "Do you live in a different reality or something?"

"As a matter of fact I do," he replied, "and you can live there too."

"The magic part of this process?" I pondered. "Are you going to teach me to be a magician?"

"Jonathan, the magical part of this process will let you achieve goals far greater than you can imagine, and there is no hocus pocus involved. It can be done with a tool you already have, which you probably haven't used correctly in the past."

I finally gave up; after all, he was half of "the smartest, kindest, most caring couple in the world," as my friend Mark had shared earlier.

"I'm all ears, Zors. Help me use the tool," I said sarcastically, still feeling the sting of realizing that my life wasn't what it could be and not wanting to face it.

As soon as I said that, I regretted it. I had said it with such sarcasm that I had almost spit out the words. Zors was generously sharing time and information with me, and I was responding in a grossly inappropriate way. Fortunately, Zors started laughing. Actually, it was more like howling. He had tears rolling down his face. I guess my pronouncement was funny, but I didn't think it was *that* funny.

As Zors pulled himself together and was getting ready to continue, I suddenly realized what was going on. He was stirring me up on purpose. I didn't know why yet, but I was sure that was what he was doing and why he was laughing so hard—he knew he had succeeded!

"Did you ever hear the expression, 'necessity is the mother of invention'?" he asked, still laughing.

"Yes," I chuckled back. His laughter was contagious.

"Well, the expression is true. The reason it's valid is that the human mind, more specifically the creative subconscious, is amazing."

"Is it different than the regular subconscious?" I asked.

"Well, let's just start off by saying that they're partners; they work together based on the information the subconscious receives and can be led to believe. The creative subconscious can't be forced to respond and it can't be turned on like a light. It creates while you're in a relaxed state, without analyzing or judging, and causes us to make the quantum leaps often attributed to genius."

"This I *have* to hear!" I exclaimed.

Zors continued, "Can you recall that I told you the subconscious will serve you, no matter what?"

"Yes."

"Well, it serves you on what it *believes* you want it to do. Psychosomatic illness, for example, is really the subconscious mind believing you want to be sick."

"Now, why would anyone want to be sick?" I asked.

"Maybe that person feels guilty about something and believes he or she deserves to be sick. There are a lot of deep psychological reasons why someone's subconscious would believe he or she wants to be ill, but that's for another time. It is prevalent, but most people just aren't aware of it.

"For example, I saw an old friend of mine a while ago, and asked how he was doing. He said he was sick and tired of his job, and he looked it. 'Have you ever considered doing something else?' I asked. Like you, he told me he wanted a better life, so I began sharing the concepts we've been talking about. Later, I suggested he get together with our mutual friend, Mark Webster, to explore some ideas. Since then, he's been building a business, and plans to retire from his job when he reaches his income goal. But I don't think you're quite ready for that."

This caused my eyebrows to raise.

"Anyway," Zors continued, "your subconscious mind is your best friend, but only if it's properly programmed. If it believes you want to react in a certain way, or be a certain kind of person, it'll do whatever it can to cause it to happen—whether it's good or bad. That's why affirmations are so powerful. When the subconscious mind is convinced something is true, it feels obligated to drive you to do the things necessary to make it a reality. It is extremely capable of responding in this way. If the subconscious believes it is true, it really is true for you."

"Okay," I said, "but what about his so-called best friend—the creative subconscious?"

"Funny you should ask," he smiled. "Here is where the magic begins. If you were to affirm something over and over again that you knew wasn't true, after a while your subconscious would become stressed. Since it knows it isn't true and yet it is told, with emotion, that it is, it must either make it true or disregard it. The subconscious initially takes the easy way out by disregarding it, but after a while the constant stress of hearing it over and over again becomes too much to bear. The subconscious finally realizes that this untruth is really supposed to be true. And being your loyal servant, it must go about making it so. Sometimes it can do it, like giving you a greater awareness of landmarks, et cetera, to help your sense of direction, but sometimes it can't do it alone."

"Well, if it can't make it true, I'd get a feeling of depression, wouldn't I?" I asked.

"Great question with excellent insight," he replied. "You would think so, but remember how totally committed the subconscious is. It will never give up; it finds a way to make it happen. It often does this by calling on its brilliant partner, the creative subconscious!"

"Brilliant partner?" I asked. "Remember Zors, this is my mind we're talking about here."

"Yes, and it is brilliant because the process makes it so," Zors answered, ignoring my weak attempt at humor. "Remember when we talked about using only five to ten percent of your mind? Well, here's where you're encouraging your mind to draw on that other ninety percent. This is how you open up the brilliance within you. I assure you, Jonathan, you won't believe how creative you are until you start utilizing this process. If you think your internal receiver's tuner was active before, wait until you unleash this. The information and ideas that will come flying into your mind will blow you away!"

"Okay, I'm psyched," I said. "How do I get started?"

"Getting started takes us back to our goals," Zors explained. "The way you set your goals using this process is completely foreign to any method you've ever been taught. For starters, you don't worry about whether a specific goal is feasible or not. Obviously, your conscious mind wouldn't believe you can reach an impossible goal. The creative subconscious, however, makes the impossible possible!

"Simply turn your desire or challenge over to it by stating what you want it to do, then relax with it. Some people do this by saying they're going to sleep on it. Then when they awake in the morning, and without any additional effort, the answer becomes clear. Others get these answers and sudden insights while doing mindless activities like showering or walking. Writers, songwriters, inventors, and such are often cited as geniuses because of their ability to tap into their creative subconscious."

"So I'm supposed to set an impossible goal?" I asked.

"Only what may seem impossible to you now. With this process, however, nothing is impossible. That's where the seemingly magical part takes over."

"Slow down, Zors, you're losing me," I said.

"Just because your conscious mind believes something's impossible doesn't mean it is! It knows only a fraction of what your subconscious does. Everything you have ever heard, seen, smelled, tasted, felt, or thought is stored there. Imagine the information that's stored in yours. Even information you sensed while you were sleeping is there. Your conscious mind uses whatever it can draw from the subconscious, but that's puny— maybe five to ten percent. This is a method to draw on more of that vast storehouse, while, at the same time, getting your internal receiver tuned into the quest. What a combination!"

"So, I set an impossible goal, and then what happens?" I asked.

"Affirm it out loud, two or three times a day, as if you've already achieved it. For example, affirm 'I'm a millionaire.' Write it down and post it everywhere. Start thinking and acting *as if* you are a millionaire! Every day, do what millionaires do: write down and prioritize your goals, act on them, read from a positive book, develop more win-win relationships, and increase your productivity by using your time and money more wisely.

"When you affirm you're a millionaire, with emotion, your subconscious goes out of its mind. *(Zors thought this was funny!)* At first, it won't believe you, so you need to say it over and over again—with emotion! Convince your subconscious that it's urgent and important. If you don't get emotional, you're demonstrating that it doesn't really matter to you."

"But how can I get emotional about it?" I interrupted.

"Listen to inspiring music; a song like *The Impossible Dream*, for instance," Zors explained. "Music can have a far-reaching impact on your emotions. Tear up when you think about being a millionaire and all the good you can do; feel it in the depths of your soul. Eventually, your subconscious accepts the affirmation and believes you *have to* be a millionaire. At that point, it will call on your creative subconscious, which helps make it a reality."

"Wow! What do I need to do next, Zors?"

"Write down ten affirmations. Word them carefully, as the subconscious will take them literally. Don't say I can do something; say it as if it's already a reality. Saying 'I can lose 20 pounds' does nothing—your subconscious already knows you can; you've changed nothing. Saying 'I weigh 170 pounds,' when you're 190 involves the creative subconscious. Its creativity kicks in to help you create what you're affirming. Just remember to get emotional about it!"

"Zors, I can't thank you enough. I'm excited and I'll get right to work on it. Thank you so much."

"You're welcome. I'm right next door if you need me."

"There are people who live to be angry. There are people who live to be victims. They are continually affirming negative input into their sub-consciouses. Their self-talk is poisoning their minds, bodies, and lives."

—Zors

—Chapter 10—

Coming to Fruition

The next month of my life was a busy one, and I saw Zors only briefly in passing. I was religiously working with my affirmations and I saw my world changing. I was attracting information, people, and possibilities beyond my wildest imagination. I was very excited about this amazing new tool as it was quite obvious that it was beginning to work. I wasn't sleeping well, however, so I thought I'd better talk to Zors about it. Finally, I got the chance.

"So how's everything going?" he asked one day when we both happened to see each other.

"Good things seem to be happening most every day. How about you?"

"Oh, I'm thankful, as always," said Zors. "But are you still working with your affirmations?"

That seemed like a very strange question. He knew how fantastic this process was; why would he think I'd try it for a short time and then quit?

"Of course I am," I answered. "They're already impacting my life. Why would you think I might have given up already?"

"Everyone doesn't necessarily find the process of value," he said.

"How could that be? I've experienced significant positive change already."

"It's quite puzzling," Zors said. "Some people use the process their whole lives and experience wonderful results, while others just stop—sometimes right before a big breakthrough. I have a few theories about why this happens, but I'm not really sure."

"What are your theories?" I asked.

"Well, first of all, some people don't use the process correctly. When they don't get significant results quickly, they figure it's a waste of time."

"How do you use this process incorrectly?" I asked.

"There are basically four ways to neutralize the program. The first, as we discussed, is to say you *can* do something. The subconscious hears the *can* and perceives that as giving you a *choice* whether or not to make it happen. Saying 'I can do it' is worse than 'I'll try!' It's *not* a commitment to do it. The second error is to get so used to saying the words of the affirmation, that you stop actively thinking about their meaning. This makes the process a waste of time. Not using emotion is yet another mistake. And finally, not saying the affirmations regularly means they're not that important to you."

"But if you're doing everything correctly, you would surely continue, wouldn't you?" I asked hopefully.

"Not necessarily," he said. "Some people prefer being right rather than being happy or successful."

"What does that mean?"

"Well, let's say I did something to harm you, something so bad that you were furious with me. You would have a right to be angry. What I did was terrible. You're justified. That anger, however, will not serve you well. Holding onto it will make you unhappy; it can even make you sick. You know this, but you feel so justified in your anger that you hang onto it anyway. You choose to be right rather than happy or well.

"Now there are people who live to be angry. There are people who live to be victims. They are continually affirming negative input into their subconsciouses. Their self-talk is poisoning their minds, bodies, and lives. They are in a habit which takes serious effort to break.

"If you encounter a deeply depressed person and can get him to change his negative self-talk into positive self-talk, you go a long way toward relieving him of his depression. But getting someone to repeat a few affirmations each day, while at the same time burying himself in negative self-talk, just won't work."

"So self-talk is a form of affirming?" I asked.

"Absolutely, in the purest form. Remember when I told you this was a tool you have been using for a long time? Well, the next part of this process is actively changing your self-talk. Your self-talk can undo your affirmations. If you continue to affirm you are happy, while your self-talk complains about how unhappy you are, guess what? You have neutralized the process."

I was speechless for a moment. "Then there's more to this process than just affirming a few times a day? Why didn't you tell me that?"

"The last time we talked, you kind of terminated the conversation," he said. "The little light went on, you felt you had a grasp on what I was saying, and that was that. But there's so much more I can tell you."

"I apologize," I said. "I thought you were through and I had it all."

"Well, you had an important piece, but there's more. No harm done. We just don't want to take our whole lives to get to everything. So tell me, how are your affirmations going?"

"The affirmations are absolutely helping me change my life in a positive new way. With this powerful tool, I know I can accomplish anything. I feel as if I'm finally in charge of my life."

—Jonathan Weatherby

—Chapter 11—

Ah, Sleep, Sweet Sleep...

"**Z**ors, I'm thrilled at what's happening in my life. The affirmations are absolutely helping me change my life in a positive new way. The best part is my locus of control has gone from external to internal. With this powerful tool, I know I can accomplish anything. I feel as if I'm *finally* in charge of my life!"

"So you have a better outlook on life," he said, obviously pleased. "That's great. Any problems?"

"Actually there is a problem," I said. "I'm not sleeping too well, and I'm tired all the time. It could be because I'm so excited about this process."

"What about using an affirmation to help you with the problem?" he asked.

"Well, I started out with an affirmation to give me increased energy, but it doesn't seem to be working."

"What is it?"

"Okay, this is exactly what I'm saying: *From the moment I wake up until I go to sleep at night, I have an abundance of positive mental and physical energy.*

"I've always had trouble sleeping, so I thought this would help me during the day."

Zors smiled broadly. "I think I can help. First, let me ask you a few questions."

"Okay," I said.

"When you say you have trouble sleeping, what exactly do you mean by that? Do you have trouble falling asleep? Do you wake up often throughout the night? Or do you wake up and then can't get back to sleep?"

"All of the above," I quipped.

"Really?"

"Well, not totally. I have a lot of trouble falling asleep, but I normally don't keep waking up. However, when I do wake up, I can't seem to go back to sleep—that seems to be new."

"How about caffeine intake?" he asked.

"I don't consume any caffeine after noon. I started this about a year ago and I guess it helps a little."

"First of all, you need to change your affirmation," he said.

"Why?"

"Because you use the phrase 'from the moment I wake up.' You might want to change that to 'the moment I start my day.' You have programmed yourself to have an abundance of positive energy the moment you wake up. If you wake up in the middle of the night, for whatever reason, you're going to receive a burst of energy—that's not what you really want. Be careful what you wish for; you might get it. Be careful what you affirm; you'll probably get it."

What he said made perfect sense. "So when you warned me about wording the affirmations carefully, you weren't kidding."

"Right," Zors responded. "As long as your self-talk doesn't contradict it and you take appropriate action, what you affirm does eventually happen and in *exactly* the way you say it. Remember, affirmations need to be one positive sentence, starting with 'I,' in the present tense, filled with emotion, and worded exactly as you want things to be.

"Alright, we know you can fix part of the problem by changing that affirmation; so let's discuss the rest of it. When you wake up in the middle of the night, what do you think about?"

"I think about what I have to do during the day," I answered. "Actually, I come up with some pretty good ideas in the middle of the night."

"Do you look at the clock?"

"Sure."

"Okay, Jonathan, we can overcome the challenges. I've spent a great deal of time studying how the mind works."

Zors continued. "Let's talk about brain activity. Right now, in an alert state, your brain is quite active. When you're asleep, its activity slows down. It's possible to control your brain to some degree to create different levels of activity."

"So, then, are you normally asleep when the brain activity is slower?" I asked.

"Well, it's pretty hard to be awake when your brain activity is in the sleep mode, but I suppose it's possible. There are times when you're awake, but in a very relaxed and calm mental state, when your brain activity slows to near-sleep levels."

"So, if I could slow my brain way down, I could be in deep sleep. That's what I want, isn't it?"

"Yes and no," Zors answered. "But since I don't want to get too technical, let's just discuss getting to sleep and staying asleep."

"Okay," I said, "but I have to tell you this is interesting stuff. Just let me ask one more question first though. Other than being in an extremely calm mental state, are there other times when you are awake but very mentally relaxed?"

"Sure, many times, like when you are mesmerized by something. For example, you are alone in a quiet room picturing yourself on the beach and feeling the warm sun caressing your face.

"When you are mentally relaxed, your subconscious is more susceptible to suggestion because the conscious mind is 'in the background.' And you already know how powerful your subconscious is."

I flashed back to Mark's edification of the Zors couple, especially my experience with Zors. Maybe Mark was right. I mean, who would know all this stuff and care enough to share it with others? We start talking about my inability to sleep well, and he explains how it all works. Incredible!

"So how do I sleep better, Zors?"

"First, when you lie down at night and begin thinking about what you're going to do the next day, you're keeping your brain active. Therefore, you won't fall asleep. When you wake up in the middle of the night and start thinking, you don't fall back to sleep because you're keeping your brain active. Just the act of looking at the clock when you wake up, puts your brain back into active mode. You're actively thinking about how much more time you can sleep before you have to get up."

"Wow, this is fascinating," I said. "Are you *sure* about all of this?"

"Yes," he said.

"Anyway," he continued, "to slow your mind down, concentrate on relaxing each part of your body, going from head to toe. For example, start with 'My hair is relaxing and falling asleep.' Your mind will continue to tempt you to think about other things, but don't let that happen. Just concentrate on relaxing your body and ignore the conscious mind. Do this and make sure you change that affirmation right away. You'll start to sleep a lot better."

I thanked Zors and went home. I just couldn't get over his depth of knowledge. I knew there was a lot more to learn from him, and I wasn't going to be shy anymore about asking.

"As long as your self-talk doesn't contradict it and you take appropriate action, what you affirm does eventually happen and in exactly *the way you say it*. Remember, affirmations need to be one positive sentence, starting with 'I,' in the present tense, filled with emotion, and worded exactly as you want things to be."

—Zors

*"**O**vercoming challenges is what makes us successful, and you need to understand that. It may not be easy to accept this idea while going through a difficult time, but accepting it is essential if one is to fully benefit from the challenge."*

—Zors

—Chapter 12—

The Gift of Challenges

One day, I was talking to Zors about my brother. "He's very unhappy. Most of his discontent emanates from his unhappiness with his job and he can't stand his boss. The guy is ineffective, dishonest, not to mention mean, and is making it impossible for my brother to continue working there much longer."

"That's good," Zors responded.

"What are you talking about?" I retorted in shock. "I just told you how unhappy he is. I thought you cared about people!"

Zors smiled, "I do care. That's why I said 'That's good!' Let me tell you a little story. One day, a tuna went into a neighborhood diner and hopped up onto a stool at the counter. The server, acting as if this happened every day, said, 'Hey, fella, we have a salad named after you,' to which the tuna replied, "So you have a salad named *Tony*?'"

I just stared at Zors, "You don't want to talk about my brother, do you?"

"Not really," he said. "So he has a challenge; that's no big deal. We all have challenges and that's a good thing."

"How can challenges be a good thing?" I asked, really getting frustrated at this point. "My brother is a great guy, a loving family man, and an excellent employee, but he's miserable at work, which is overshadowing his entire life."

"Alright," Zors sighed, "your question deserves an answer. There are so many levels to this; I honestly don't know where to start."

I didn't say a word; I could see the wheels turning in Zors' head and I knew I was going to learn something valuable. I just waited.

"Challenges are wonderful gifts," he began. "Overcoming them is what makes us successful, and you need to understand that. It may not be easy to accept this idea while going through a difficult time, but accepting it is essential if one is to fully benefit from the challenge."

Zors stopped talking for what seemed like a long time. I interrupted the silence. "You *are* going to continue, aren't you? Not to be disrespectful, Zors, but so far you aren't making any sense."

"A tuna went into a diner."

"Zors," I pleaded, "stop driving me crazy."

"Okay," Zors laughed. "Let me tell you all the ways that challenges are really blessings."

"This ought to be good," I said, doubtfully.

"If we didn't have any challenges," he went on, "life would be quite boring. Imagine how dull it would be if we could never experience the great feeling of accomplishment that comes when we overcome a challenge.

"Challenges separate the men from the boys—the strong from the weak. Successful people find a way to deal with and overcome their challenges; unsuccessful people allow themselves to be defeated by them. But it's just a choice. Unsuccessful people often ignore their challenges, hoping they'll go away. But when challenges aren't dealt with, they fester and can eventually overwhelm and consume the person, creating a real mess.

"Challenges are carriers; they *always* bring special gifts. The bigger the challenge, the greater the gift. You may not see this when you are in the midst of working through a challenge; but if you went back and reviewed your most difficult times, you would realize the gifts were just wonderful. Once you understand that something good is going to come out of it, even while you are in the thick of it, you'll be on your way to greater success and happiness. Now, of course, this is only true if you don't quit. I could cite dozens of examples, but I'll give you just one.

"Many years ago, when Ruth and I were first married, her mother became bedridden with emphysema. Her father retired from his job to take care of her full-time. Shortly thereafter, he died from a sudden heart attack. We were young with little money. We couldn't afford to hire someone to take care of her, so we moved into her house to care for her ourselves.

"There is a Chinese symbol for a home: a roof with a skirt underneath it. The symbol for war, however, is two skirts under one roof—two women in the same house. And that's how it was in this case. Ruth's mother was difficult to begin with, but coping with her additional orneriness from being sick, and her rebellion at having her daughter in charge, was pure agony.

"I made a promise to myself when we moved in, to never argue with Ruth's mom. After all, she was ill, we were living in her house, and she had just lost her husband. Keeping that promise was the hardest task I ever took on, but somehow I did it. She gave me every reason to break my promise, but I answered her baiting with love and affection.

"As all this was going on, I tried to determine what blessing was hidden in this difficult time. Ruth was constantly arguing with her mother and our lives were turned upside down. I could perceive no blessing.

"Well, her mom died about a year after we had moved in. At the funeral, all her sisters thanked me for taking such good care of her. They said she had told them I was wonderful to her. I was amazed, but that wasn't the real blessing.

"About six months later, I was reexamining the experience. Something had happened to me during that year. I wasn't a patient person before, but that experience helped me develop more patience than I could have ever imagined. The challenge of learning patience with my ornery mother-in-law had helped me form a new habit.

"Second, and more importantly, Ruth and I grew closer. We had to bond more closely together over that difficult time, just to get through it with our sanity intact. That closeness, which is still growing, was and is a lifelong blessing."

As I listened intently to Zors, it was as if a light went on in my head, "Boy, I guess there *is* something to be said for challenges," I observed.

"Oh, I haven't told you the best part," he responded thoughtfully. "Challenges are also wonderful change agents."

"What do you mean by that?" I asked.

"Real challenges always involve emotions and decisions requiring change. These decisions are usually made mostly based on emotions, not logic, as many may think."

"Are you sure?" I asked, still uncertain where all this was leading.

"Yes, now let me tell you about my business."

"No, Zors, would you please stay on subject?" I pleaded, once again. "With all due respect, I'm confused. It seems you do this purposely to make me crazy."

"I *am* staying on the subject," he said. "I *am* endeavoring to teach you something. God knows it isn't easy."

Of course, it was always nice to learn something more from Zors. I admire him from the bottom of my heart. I could be perfectly honest with him and humor him and he would give it right back to me. The great part was that even though he knew so much, he never took himself too seriously. He was as humble as they came and patient as well.

"Some people who get into their own business," he continued, "aren't really serious about their dream and, therefore, don't really apply themselves. They don't understand how a business really works. For instance, they may believe that the lowest price always wins the day, but if that were so, we'd all be driving the same car—the cheapest one!

For example, our products and services aren't always the least expensive, yet we have one of the biggest businesses in the community. In fact, our business is so good that we have been able to expand it to many parts of the nation as well as the world. 'Why?' you may ask. The truth is, my business is simple. But like anything else worthwhile, building it requires focus, enthusiasm, and commitment. It revolves around creating and maintaining mutually beneficial relationships—caring about others and helping them get what they want—which gives you what you want.

"At the same time, every one of my people has come to me at some point with the 'stupid prospect' excuse. This is where the business owner uses logic to show the potential client or associate why he or she needs our products, services, or opportunity, but they *still* say no. My people typically tell me that the prospect had to be stupid; they said no even though they hadn't been offered anything better.

"Well, the prospect didn't remain a prospect because he was stupid. He didn't take action because he wasn't moved to do so. There was no emotion, or at least not sufficient emotion involved to cause him to make a change. Most people like the status quo because they don't like change. How many people stay in jobs they dislike or even hate, and other undesirable situations—until someone or something makes it emotionally impossible for them to remain in the status quo?

"Do you think people typically get married because it makes sense *logically*? For a huge life change like that, emotion needs to be involved. That's why most people get married—they're in love. It's an emotion!"

"So you teach your people how to get the prospect to love them?" I jokingly asked.

"Not quite. Business owners need to find an area of dissatisfaction with the prospect's current situation. Once they discover the 'pain,' they use it to get the prospect to realize they need to make a change. The logical part of the presentation is there so the prospect can understand how it all makes sense—especially for those prospects who are analytically inclined."

Zors paused for a while to collect his thoughts. "Challenges are among our greatest blessings," he said. "They force us to make the changes that we need to make. They are the stones by which we sharpen ourselves. All challenges are accompanied by wonderful gifts, which sometimes take a while for us to discover. Your brother is very lucky to have such a big challenge."

"Good stuff, Zors," I said. "I don't think I will ever perceive challenges the same way again."

"I'll be sure to remind you of that if you ever come crying to me again!" Zors concluded.

"I'm sure you will. Thanks, Zors."

"*Challenges are among our greatest blessings. They force us to make the changes that we need to make. They are the stones by which we sharpen ourselves. All challenges are accompanied by wonderful gifts, which sometimes take a while for us to discover.*"

—Zors

"Reprogramming my mind was like discovering a new part of me I never knew existed!"

—Jonathan Weatherby

—Chapter 13—

It's Been There All Along...

My life was rapidly changing for the better. When Zors initially told me how powerful my mind was, I was skeptical. It wasn't that I didn't believe him; I just didn't realize the level of accomplishment one could attain by properly programming his or her mind.

The most dramatic and noticeable part of the process was with the internal receiver. I was moving in a positive direction, and I knew the affirmations were responsible. But I never expected such a dramatic change in the information I was noticing. It was very different from what I had experienced in the past, and it was all very exciting. I had perceived the world differently. I finally understood that what I was looking for in life was right in front of me—thanks to Zors!

I started experimenting with the affirmations. I remembered Mark telling me that the process had helped him improve his golf game, so I decided I would give it a go. I began affirming, "I'm an excellent golfer and hit the ball so it will land exactly where I want it to." In a short time, my golf game began to improve, but I wasn't sure why. It didn't take long, though, before I got a hint of what was happening.

Every summer for several years, I'd been playing golf with friends on Saturday mornings. They were all much better players than me. Nonetheless, we really enjoyed each other's company. After I started the affirmation to improve my game, I began perceiving our Saturday morning outings differently.

"One day, I was standing behind my friend, Allen, when he teed up the ball. I noticed he had found a place on the tee where the ball was higher than his feet. This would create the tendency to pull the ball to the left. After he hit it, I asked him if he had purposely set it up that way.

"Sure," he said, "there were woods along the right side, so I wanted to protect against 'pushing' the ball to the right. I use that strategy all the time."

He uses that strategy all the time? I'd been playing golf with him for years and never noticed it! But since I'm now affirming that I'm a better golfer, I immediately notice and learn new strategies. It is obvious to where my internal receiver is now tuned.

On another day, I was driving home from attending a seminar. The speaker had made a point about temporary employment agencies and how our society had become one of constant job changes, and that most people didn't like their work or some aspect surrounding it. He also said that one of the temp agencies had more employees than any other company in the country.

For some reason, as I was thinking about his presentation, I just couldn't seem to remember the name of that company. It bothered me to the point where I started saying out loud: "I can't think of the name of the company, I can't think of the name of the company."

All of a sudden, I heard one of Zors' earlier comments in my head: "Now there's an affirmation that will serve you well."

My self-talk; I had to watch my self-talk! I immediately changed the affirmation to: "I remember the name of the company," and, almost immediately, it came to me!

It wasn't so amazing that I remembered the name; it was *how* I remembered it. I suddenly saw the whiteboard the speaker had used at the seminar: He had written the company's name on it. That wasn't my normal way of remembering; I had never remembered anything in that way before. I knew it was because I was reprogramming my mind, but it was like discovering a part of me I never knew existed!

As time went on, Zors and I became closer and closer. I just loved the times when we got together and talked. I would always learn something important and often have a good laugh. Zors could find humor in almost anything, and he used it to help me relax. He made learning and growing fun things to do.

"**B**e excited every day. We all have days when we just don't feel like being productive, when it would be much easier to just coast. These are the days when you have to reach deep down inside and find a way to make the day count— then do it."

—Zors

—Chapter 14—

Five Percenters Make Things Happen!

O ne day I finally asked Zors: "How did you come to the conclusion that five percent of the people drive the world, while ninety-five percent go along for the ride? Why isn't it six or eight percent; why five?"

"My life insurance agent taught me this," Zors explained. "He told me about a study which had been conducted by the American Bankers Association. They examined the financial success of men in the United States by focusing on their working lives. If you were to ask a hundred twenty-five-year-old men if they want to achieve financial success, it's pretty safe to assume they'd all say yes. Now I suppose you could get one or two to say no, but that wouldn't be a normal response. They used men, by the way, because men were generally more career-oriented during the time of the survey.

"Anyway, what happens to these men over the next forty years? The numbers might be a bit different by now, but that study showed that thirty-six of them died before they reached sixty-five. Of the remaining group; one was deemed wealthy, four were financially independent, five had to keep working, and fifty-four were dependant upon someone else to support them. So if you added up all the figures—thirty-six are dead, fifty-four are dependant on others, and five are still working—you find that ninety-five of the original one-hundred reached age sixty-five dead or dead broke. That, by the way, is in the richest country in the world! So, if you pattern your life after everyone around you, you have ninety-five chances out of a hundred of being a financial failure. You just can't live your life like they do and reasonably expect financial success."

"And you think those numbers are still valid?" I asked.

"I think there are certain similarities among five percent of the population that helps them lead more successful lives. I'm talking about overall success, not just financial well-being, and, of course, people define success differently. The more I study people, the more I know this is true. That doesn't mean that the ninety-five percent can't be happy or that the five percent don't have their share of difficulties; I'm talking about life achievements."

"So the five percenters have a whole list of similarities?" I inquired curiously.

"You're fishing for the list, aren't you?" he asked, smiling. "Well, they all don't have all the same attributes. I do believe, though, that there are a few they must have in common. For example, they all exhibit a powerful internal locus of control, where they take responsibility for their own lives. Systematically or not, they all practice positive affirmations while never giving themselves any negative self-talk. Of course they have other similar traits that give them advantages over those in the ninety-five percent group."

Zors stopped talking for a minute and mentally seemed to "go away." I was patiently waiting for him to start again but I was too excited to wait any longer.

"Zors, come back to me, please," I finally said. "Are you coming back to earth soon?"

"I'm sorry," he responded. "I drifted back in time momentarily. I was always so stubborn; I was endeavoring to recall how I was able to open myself up to this information in the first place. When I was a young man, I thought I knew everything and had all the answers."

"Some very strong emotional event must have opened your eyes to new information," I offered.

Zors smiled at me. "That's exactly right."

"Well, what was it?"

"Do you want to know what else the five percenters have in common or don't you?" he barked, abruptly switching gears.

"Sure," I said. I must have touched a nerve.

Zors softened and began to focus again. "Successful people are prepared for the big game. They are prepared for the divisional championship, and they are prepared for the Superbowl!"

"What are you talking about?" I asked. Zors seemed to love it when I appeared totally lost. I knew he was setting me up for an important point, but sometimes I just responded this way for his amusement.

Zors resisted the urge to laugh. "Can you be patient enough for me to make a point or two?"

"Go ahead," I conceded, feeling like a two-year-old squirming in his seat.

Zors continued, "Did you ever hear the name Mike Milkovich?"

"Sure," I said. "He was a wrestling coach at Maple Heights High School for years."

"That's like saying Seabiscuit was just a racehorse," Zors replied. "Milkovich is a legend in this community. He won fifteen state championships in his tenure and God knows how many second places. Unbelievable for a small community school that had to wrestle against large public schools, and parochial schools that could attract top wrestlers by offering scholarships."

"You're trying to lose me again, Zors," I quipped.

"No, think about it. Do you want to just play around or talk about success and how Mike could have achieved such a record?" Zors asked, faking sternness.

"Maybe he was just a good coach," I suggested.

"And maybe getting man to walk on the moon was a walk in the park," he wittily responded. "Good coach?" he hollered. "That guy was a miracle worker! I had to discover what his secret was as part of my search for success, and I finally got the opportunity.

"One day, his son, Mike, Jr., came calling to sell me something. He had been an excellent wrestler as had all the Milkovich boys. I got to know the kid a little and finally asked him the question. I said I knew his father was a superior coach technically, but was that the reason for his dad's spectacular success? Here's what Mike Jr. told me:

"'Before every practice, my father would take ten minutes to talk to the team. He would tell us something different every day; something that really inspired us. After his ten minutes, the team was so fired up that they practiced seriously. There was no horsing around or anything like that. All you could see and hear were wrestlers working very hard, preparing for their upcoming matches. You see, it's easy to get psyched up at the time of your match; everybody does that. If you aren't prepared, however, it doesn't matter. My dad got everyone psyched up in the preparation stage, so we always outprepared our opponents. That was Dad's secret!'"

"So preparation is one of the attributes?" I asked.

"Yes, but preparation is made up of two parts: First, look ahead and have the proper tools to deal with future situations—not just what will probably occur, but what *could also* happen as well. Second, be excited every day. We all have days when we just don't feel like being productive, when it would be much easier to just coast. These are the days when you have to reach deep down inside and find a way to make the day count—then do it."

"What about those days when something devastating happens?" I asked. "Or what about when I'm sick? Am I supposed to be productive on *those* days too? Can't I *ever* take a break?"

"Sure," Zors said admonishingly. "Those in the ninety-five percent group find reasons to take breaks all the time. They're called excuses."

"Come on, Zors," I said. "There are times in life when you can be completely knocked for a loop. There are days when it just seems too hard to get up and get going."

Zors stared right through me. "Remember our conversation about the gift of challenges? Keep in mind, the finest steel goes through the hottest fire. There are times when you have to muster the courage to keep going, when all you have left in you is the will to do so. That's what five percenters do!"

"I know you're right, Zors," I conceded. "I'm sure the ability to force yourself to press on when others say they can't—or won't—separates the winners from the losers."

"Yes, it really does, Jonathan. Your response to challenges reveals a great deal about you."

"Then preparedness is paramount to getting the job done, no matter what the hurdles are?" I reiterated.

"Remember the part about being prepared for perceived future situations?" Zors continued. "Anyone who has ever played serious chess will tell you that the best players are always many moves ahead in their planning. The same is true in the game of life."

"Got it," I said.

"Good, and remember Hemmingway's definition of courage—'grace under pressure.'"

"If you really want to communicate with someone in a truly meaningful way, use emotion. Coupling this with focusing on his or her dreams will often elevate the relationship to a new level."

—Zors

Chapter 15

More of What Five Percenters Do...

A few days later, I was able to catch Zors alone, basically with some free time. He was washing one of his cars, a job he normally delegated, which meant I had a captive audience.

"Why didn't you take the car over to the local car wash? Do you have a lot of free time or are you just saving money?" I asked.

"I'm fresh out of change but you can wash it with me," he countered with a wink.

"Sure, I'll help you and keep you company. Throw me a sponge."

Zors laughed. "Lucky me, what do you *really* want?"

"Well, you shortchanged me," I said as I sudsed up the front of the car. "The last time we talked, you didn't finish the list of the similar characteristics of the five percenters. You got me so fired up about preparedness, I lost my focus and left without hearing the rest."

"You know, I really like you, Jonathan, although I would like you even more if you enjoyed washing cars as a hobby.

What's really nice in teaching you some of these methodologies is that it reminds me to use them. There's no better way to learn something and make it a part of you than to teach it to others. Affirmations are excellent tools for forming positive habits, but nothing is quite as effective as teaching."

"That's fine, Zors," I said impatiently. "Maybe someday I'll be a leader. Right now, though, I'd love to hear the rest of the list."

"Alright," Zors said, "there are two more concepts that I'll share with you. Then, you'll know everything I know! Will you still come and visit with me after that?"

All of a sudden I felt guilty and selfish. "Oh, my goodness, Zors, I don't spend time with you just to greedily obtain information. I really like you and care about you. I love just spending time with you."

"That's okay, Jonathan," he said. "I'm only demonstrating a concept. I know you spend time with me because we are friends. I greatly value our time together as well.

"The reason I phrased my question that way was to demonstrate something important regarding the ability to communicate effectively. When I asked you if you would still visit with me, I introduced emotion into our conversation. It worked, didn't it? Once again, emotion is a critical piece of the powerful methodology I taught you. The ability to communicate in a highly effective manner to yourself and others is extremely important. Poor communication is how my brother broke his back."

"Good heavens!" I exclaimed. "What happened?"

"We were moving a piano up a flight of stairs. He hollered 'heave ho' and I thought he said 'leave go.'"

"Zors, that's not funny!" I yelled. "You scared me!"

Zors just laughed and continued, "The ability to communicate on an emotional level can help a person with integrity develop strong, mutually advantageous relationships very quickly."

"Why does it have to be a person with integrity?" I asked sophomorically.

"Because you can't fake concern," he answered. "If you have unkind, unfair motives, no technique on earth is going to fool people for long. If you honestly care about others, however, you can use certain basic principles to begin relationships so you can become friends and assist them. You do it all the time. Just smiling when you meet someone sends a positive message. Remembering names pays dividends in a far greater proportion than the effort needed to do so. And the quickest and most enduring method of forming a personal relationship is appealing to one's passion, one's dream.

"Everyone has something they love to do. There are so many tasks in life we have to do, but there are also those which we want to do or do more of. Maybe it's spending more time with the kids. Some people collect dolls, coins, antiques, cars, all kinds of stuff. I love playing golf. Most everybody has something he or she is passionate about, above and beyond their work. Once you know a person's passion or dream, you have an important key with which to communicate with that person."

"You mean like talking golf with you?" I asked.

"Well, that's an oversimplification. Here's what I mean: Let's say you meet someone with whom you want to develop a relationship. Let's also assume you begin doing business with this man. In the course of everyday conversation, you discover he loves to watch baseball with his son. In addition to that, you discover that his son's favorite player is Omar Visquel. Since Omar does a lot of public appearances in Cleveland, and you're always out meeting new people anyway, you figure you might as well go. But this time you invite the man, his wife, and his son to accompany you and your wife, who's your business partner. Now what do you think happens?"

"Well, I'm sure the guy and his family would be very surprised and thankful," I replied.

"Yes, but it would be more than that. The fact that you knew what was really important to him and invited him and his family along to meet Omar was very thoughtful. The point is the act of doing all this *changes the relationship.* When you really care about someone and do something nice for that person, you both feel good about it. But when your caring act includes his or her passion or the passion of someone he or she loves, it leaves an indelible mark."

"That would be dramatic," I admitted, "but how do you discover someone's passion without probing into his personal life?"

"It's not like that," Zors replied. "All you need to do is ask someone what he or she really enjoys doing in his or her free time, or what they'd like to do most, and they'll tell you. People *love* to talk about their passions. When you ask the question be prepared to hear, in detail, what they love to do, how they do it, when they do it, and so forth. You'll actually see the passion on his or her face and hear it in that person's voice.

"Remember, if you really want to communicate with someone in a truly meaningful way, use emotion. Coupling this with focusing on his or her dream will often elevate the relationship to a new level."

"Great stuff, Zors. As long as you are on a roll, what was the other point you were going to share with me?"

"What do you mean?" he asked.

"You said there were two concepts; the emotional communication concept is one, but what's the other?"

"Oh," Zors responded, "the other is to accomplish twice as much every day as the average person. Well, I guess we're not going to get this car much cleaner. Thanks for your help. I think I'll go inside now."

"Come on, Zors. You can't leave on that note. How do I accomplish twice the average?"

"Okay," he said, "but this technique is so simple that I'm afraid you won't take it seriously."

"I'll take it seriously, if it works," I said.

"Oh, it works alright. You'll double your productivity. This is a very powerful tool."

"Well, if you said it, if it came out of your mouth, it must be true," I said, "and I respect that!"

Zors laughed. "Okay, here it is. Each evening, simply make a list of every task you want to complete the next day, putting the list in priority order. The next day, work on task one until it's done. Don't go on to task two until task one is completed. Then cross it off your list and go on to task two. Follow this procedure through the entire list, not going on to the next task until the present one is done. The only time you can move on from a task that isn't done is when something beyond your control keeps you from finishing it. Then do whatever you can—make a call to get information, schedule an appointment, or write yourself a note to pick something up. Do whatever you can toward completion of the task. Then, move on until you have what you need to go back and finish the incomplete task."

"That's it?" I asked.

"That's it," he replied.

"No big deal, I can do that."

Zors frowned. "You seem to be taking my advice rather lightly," he growled.

"Come on, Zors," I replied, "that list thing is not too exciting."

"Not too exciting, eh? It's only the most powerful organizational tool known to man!"

"How can that be?" I asked.

Zors was really fired up and shot back, "You tell me how that could possibly be. For once, think through what I just told you and explain to me why it's so powerful."

Zors wasn't kidding. I had to figure this one out and fast. "Well, it's a good way to organize yourself," I offered feebly.

"Duh," Zors groaned.

"It's also an excellent planning tool," I added.

"Double duh," Zors groaned once more.

"So what's the answer, Zors? I honestly don't know," I said weakly.

"Yes, you do. Now think about it."

I thought for a while, but the pressure of having to come up with the right answer was blocking the process. "So, I guess it makes you work by priority," I said, as the light in my head finally went on.

"Good, and why is that so important?" he asked.

"Because you're getting important things done first?" I asked.

Zors chuckled. "Jonathan, I'm not going to let you off the hook. You need to realize, within yourself, why this is so powerful. Now, tell me why this 'list thing,' as you call it, is so important?"

I immediately asked myself, "If I were the teacher and Zors were the student, how would I best explain this to him?"

"This technique," I said forcefully, "is very important." Zors started laughing, not used to my new burst of confidence. "First of all it gives you a roadmap for the day."

"Good!" Zors exclaimed.

"The roadmap is special because it directs you to the most important places first. It won't let you go to the less important places until you have visited those you need to visit beforehand."

"Very good!"

I continued, "We often spend our time doing tasks we *like* to do, rather than tasks we *need* to do. As a result, we fail to accomplish our objective. Prioritizing the list helps us stay focused on investing our time in accomplishing our goals."

"Excellent," he encouraged. "Go on."

"Go on what?"

"Go on and tell me what else is important about the process."

"I don't know," I offered reluctantly.

"You really do know, or is it that you just won't think?" he barked. "Okay, I'll give you this one. This process programs your mind. Isn't that what we have been discussing forever? Not only that, focusing on your priorities also gives you peace of mind.

"When you get in the habit of always working by priority, you are miles ahead of the rest of the world. Just the act of crossing off completed tasks sends important messages to your subconscious. Get in the habit of dealing with priorities *before* they become serious challenges or dreams abandoned along the way. Sometimes we avoid priorities by working on tasks we like, or those that are easy, acting as if we're productive when we're just busy. We are, however, only fooling ourselves—as our dreams slowly slip away.

"The amazing part of the list technique is that there will be items, way down the list, that stay down there, day after day, until they finally disappear. In other words, there are projects we *think* we need to do, that we really don't need to do. They are so low in priority that, after a while, they go away by themselves."

"I understand now, Zors. Thanks."

"Great! But you'll *really* understand when you actually start using it. Your productivity and peace of mind will astound you."

"I believe you, Zors. I really believe you," I said smiling.

"The more you share, the more you receive; and it's all out of proportion to what you share. It's absolutely amazing!"

—Zors

—Chapter 16—

The Magic of Sharing

Within a few months, I had quickly evolved, in many ways, into a different person. The affirmations and other dynamic tools had served me well. I had started building my own business in association with Mark and Zors, adopted an external locus of control, and developed a new appreciation for my blessings. Still, all was not perfect. I needed to talk to Zors and, luckily, I was able to catch up with him as he was coming back from the airport.

"Zors, have you got a minute?" I asked.

"I've got at least two for you, Jonathan," he answered, grinning.

"I need some advice on leading people because I want to go to the next level. As you know, I'm now beginning to mentor several business owners, but some of them don't seem to be taking the concept of locus of control seriously."

As Zors listened and looked at me, there was a hint of sadness in his eyes. "Are you teaching them about affirmations?" he asked.

"Yes, but some of them just aren't getting it," I lamented. "I don't seem to be able to get them to buy into the process. I know it works, but I can't get everyone to give it a go."

"I'm sorry, Jonathan," he said. "I should have warned you."

"Warned me about what?" I asked.

"Learning about affirmations, locus of control, and the other ideas we've discussed can be both beneficial and detrimental. You're growing, becoming more effective, more productive—and that's great. It's just disappointing to discover that many people, even those we love, as much as they may complain, aren't hungry enough to improve their lot in life. I totally understand what you're going through."

I was truly confused this time. "Please explain," I begged.

"It's extremely frustrating to watch people fail—especially those you care about and feel a responsibility to help. You know what Louis Armstrong used to say, don't you?"

"You mean the great trumpet player?"

"Yes. Armstrong said, 'Some people don't know and you just can't tell 'em.' This is very true, but extremely frustrating. That's why I'm so happy for you."

My mouth fell open. "Happy for me?" I gasped. "What are you talking about? I often feel guilty that I could never repay you for all you have done for me. My whole life has changed for the better. I'm a better husband, father, friend, and leader. I'm also happier and much more productive." I felt strong emotions building up inside of me, and tears of gratitude for Zors' help were welling up in my eyes.

"I appreciate your gratitude," Zors said quietly. "But there's more to it than that, Jonathan."

"Really?" I asked, having no idea where Zors was going with this.

"Let me explain. You already know about the ninety-five and the five percent. It's really challenging to find candidates for the five percent. That's one person out of twenty. Now hold that thought.

"There's a scientific law that says for every action there is an equal and opposite reaction; but there's more to it than that. Ruth taught me a long time ago that there's magic in sharing. Whatever you share is returned to you many times over. So, the more you give to others, as in sharing with them, the more you will eventually have! I know she's right because she's the smartest, most caring person I know."

I was amazed. I used to think of Ruth only as Zors' wife. She was the nicest person on the planet, but I couldn't imagine how anyone could be as intelligent as Zors, let alone more so. But then again, they were both leaders in a large international business, of which I was now a part. One night a month, dozens of cars show up at their house. I used to think it was a book club or something, but now I know better since I've joined Mark and Zors in the business.

Zors continued, "I work very hard giving off positives—empowering information and feelings to encourage others as much as I can. I want to share more than I want to receive—sharing is so gratifying. But it's kind of frustrating because you can never catch up. The more you share, the more you receive; and it's all out of proportion to what you share! It's absolutely amazing!

"Anyway, my greatest gift is my knowledge and caring about people. I'm not all that smart, but I've learned a lot about people and business, and I want to share it. The problem, of course, is that I can't effectively share it with the ninety-five percenters. What I share simply doesn't register with them—not now anyway. Maybe later. I always have hope for them. When the time is right for them, though, nothing will stand in the way of them getting it. That's why I'm so thrilled to have an eager student like you."

"Thanks," I muttered. I was beginning to get teary-eyed again.

Zors looked at me. "Do you remember early in our relationship, that you asked me why I was taking the time to share all this information with you?"

"Yes," I said.

"Well, now you know."

I pulled myself together. "Then I shouldn't waste my time sharing that information? I mean, I'm surrounded by ninety-five percenters."

"Yes, nineteen out of twenty," he chuckled. "Well, I'm sure you don't want to beat your head against the wall. Nonetheless, you need to be like Johnny Appleseed and sow lots of seeds. You never know which ones will take root. There are a lot of ninety-five percenters who can become five percenters. When you find those who are genuinely interested, carefully share the information. I say *carefully* because it's not a good idea to force it on anyone. Share what you have learned to anyone who is open to hearing it. Then help them discover the dream within themselves."

"So how do I get to the next level? How do I systematically give off more positives to other people? I mean, how can I accelerate my success?"

"That's easy," he answered. "Miracles!"

"What?"

"Miracles. Start performing miracles."

"All right, Zors," I begged. "Please explain that one."

"All loving or caring acts are miracles. At least that's what Ruth tells me; and if she says it, it's a fact."

"Honestly, I've never thought of it in that way," I responded. I could feel myself softening, as if this, somehow, was part of what was missing in my life.

"So, load up your sharing bank with small miracles," Zors continued. "Let people in front of you in traffic. Open doors and look for little ways to be of service to others. Help more people like I've been helping you. Help others discover their dreams and show them how they can make them come true. And be sure to remember your loved ones—the ones you may now be taking for granted."

"Boy," I said. "You're right, Zors. Sometimes I treat my family the worst of all."

"Well, you asked me about the second concept and I told you," he reminded me. "It may sound corny, but my goal is twelve miracles a day, and that's sharing them, not asking for them. There's an automatic reward built into the sharing of miracles. It makes life magical and incredibly fulfilling.

"Sometimes you have to give someone a thump on the head," Zors joked, as he was obviously referring to me. "No, when you're actively sharing, you forget about your own challenges. It really works! One of my daily affirmations is: *I love and care about others, and use what I've learned to serve them.* Make fun of it if you will, but it helps me as well as helping others.

I'm in the habit of serving others which makes me temporarily forget about my own challenges. You can't consciously think of two things at the same time. Of course, as we've already discussed, it's important to work and grow through our challenges—not ignore them. But, at the same time, we don't want to be worrying about them either. This affirmation and the everyday carrying out of it gets me through some very difficult times."

This was surely an eye-opener for me. First of all, I never thought of Zors as needing to do affirmations; but, of course, he wasn't successful by accident. Secondly, I was surprised to hear he ever had difficult times. It seemed that he had his life so together and was so upbeat, it just didn't compute. It was now clear to me that we're all human and we all need to work on ourselves to become the best we can be in fulfilling our purpose.

This conversation brought Zors and me even closer together. I vowed to share twelve miracles a day. Everything else he told me had worked, so why not this?

*"**P**ut yourself in a situation where you have to do what you've never done before, and you'll find a way to do it. Remember, the answer to "How?" is "Yes!" It takes courage. But also remember, you can't steal second base with one foot on first."*

—Zors

Chapter 17

Twelve Miracles a Day

Zors and Ruth, who had become our business mentors, too, never seemed to get older. As the years went by, they became even more loveable. Their circle of friends kept increasing, and their business grew even more.

"Zors, do you have portraits of Ruth and you in the attic? You two never seem to age."

"When life is exciting, Jonathan, you don't have time to get old," he said. "Ruth and I are so engaged in growing and helping others, it helps keep us young."

"In what way are you growing?" I asked. "I mean you can only make so much money or own so much stuff."

"Jonathan, we're grateful for everything we've been blessed with, but that's not what it's about. When I was younger, I used to believe that you were what you owned. Do you want to hear how I learned that was completely wrong?"

"Sure," I said. Why wouldn't I want to hear what Zors had to say? Modeling him had changed my life. In fact, I always had a notebook and pen handy to jot down what he said, so I could apply it to my business as well as to my life.

"I used to take a week off at the end of the year," he continued. "I would use the time to plan for the new year while reflecting on the past twelve months."

"Sounds like a good idea to me," I said.

"Well, sure. After all, you know how important preparedness is. But there was one exercise I would do at the end of each year that taught me a great lesson. I used to make a list of what I wanted to own by the end of the next year: a more expensive car, a Rolex watch, a bigger house, a vacation home, and such. I would also review the previous list to see what I had been able to acquire over the past year."

"So it was your way of keeping score," I said.

"Yes, that's right. After a few years of this exercise, however, I noticed something very interesting. It really didn't matter what I had acquired the previous year; the list for the coming year was always longer."

"Well, that was good, wasn't it?" I asked. "That must have been a strong motivator."

"It was. But I found something that was even more important than just achieving goals. It's what the process of doing so caused me to become along the way. As I grew, I discovered I needed a new obsession.

"That's when I decided to be obsessed by something that would help other people. I needed to be obsessed with making a greater difference in the world. That's what led to my twelve miracles a day: sharing knowledge with people who are humble and willing to learn, and other meaningful endeavors. Remember, there's one thing better than living the dream, and that's sharing it with others!

"To be a real asset to the human race, I needed to grow. I needed to develop myself so I could make a greater contribution to the world."

"So you needed to keep learning?" I asked.

"Yes, but more than that, I needed to stretch myself. That's the most effective way to grow. Put yourself in a situation where you have to do what you've never done before, and you'll find a way to do it. Remember, the answer to 'How?' is 'Yes!' It takes courage. But also remember, you can't steal second base with one foot on first.

"Jonathan, go out and make a bigger difference. Learn, grow, and care more about others, and help them achieve their dreams. Be more of a positive influence in the world, and you'll live the life of your dreams and beyond. You now have the tools; it's your responsibility to put them to good use."

"Thanks, Zors, you've made a huge difference in my life. I can't imagine rising above life's challenges and moving forward without the fabulous tools you helped me discover. I'd like to be successful like you, and have the same effect on others around the world. You'll always be my mentor, role model, and leader; but most of all, my friend." I started tearing up.

"You're more than welcome, Jonathan. It's been my pleasure seeing you develop. You've become a great friend as well, and your leadership skills have grown by leaps and bounds," he said with a smile as I was leaving.

Now reading about Zors and what he taught me is a great start, but how are you going to apply it to *your* life? You've probably already identified some new goals you'd like to accomplish. Right? So what are you waiting for?

Most successful people have a leader or mentor, like Zors; someone who's where they want to be, and can help them grow and become the best they can be. Develop an enduring friendship and wonderful things will happen. You'll have the chance to live a life few people are blessed to have—provided you stay the course. Listen to everything he or she says, ask questions, take notes, and then take action. You can't overcome a challenge with the same knowledge you had when the challenge first arose.

Quitting is not allowed! Remember, quitters never win and winners never quit. You'll create more time freedom, which you can spend with your family and use to pursue other interests. Follow your dream and it'll take you where you're supposed to go. If you're not already in a business where people care about people—where you can work with others to make your dreams come true—be sure to get into one. Associate with successful, happy people, and others who want to grow, and ignore the naysayers. Positive new relationships and a more exciting, fulfilling life can be yours.

Will your boss help you achieve your dreams?

A couple of years ago, Zors told me to go out and make a bigger difference. Fortunately, I had diligently taken notes of my meetings with him; I really wanted a better life. The wisdom he shared made such an impact on me that I began organizing the notes so I could easily share them with others. I was so excited about what I had put together that I wanted to show it to Zors. So I gave him a call.

"Hi, Zors! This is Jonathan," I said breathlessly. "I've got something exciting I'd like to share with you. May I come over now?"

"Sorry, Jonathan, I'm meeting with some folks in a few minutes. How about three o'clock?" Zors responded.

"Great! See you then." Waiting 'til three seemed like an eternity. When it finally came, my heart was pounding as I walked over to Zors' house.

"Come on in, Jonathan. What are you so excited about?" Zors asked, smiling.

"Zors, I've listened to and applied everything you've ever shared with me, and I know it all works. Remember how I always took notes whenever we met? Well, I've organized them, and I'd like to show you what I have. I think it'll enable everyone in the business to benefit from your wisdom, without your having to be with them. It'll also enable them to share your ideas with anyone else who wants a better life," I said with a lump in my throat.

"What have you got, Jonathan?" Zors asked, curiously.

"Last year, I went to my old boss at the publishing house where I used to work, handed him my notes, and asked if he could create a book from them. Well, here's what he came up with."

As I offered Zors the book, he stared silently at it for a few moments, then gently took it from my hand. "Jonathan, I don't know what to say. This is incredible!" Zors turned it over, read the back, and started tearing up, like I'd never seen him do before. He opened it up and just stood there, reading it as if he were in a trance. It was as though I wasn't even in the room. I quietly sat down on the couch and focused on his face to see what his reaction would be. He just kept nodding his head and smiling. Half an hour later, finally looking down at me, he broke the silence.

"This is phenomenal, Jonathan! I'd like to finish it, but based on what I've read so far, sharing this with business owners and others who want a better life could cause tremendous growth in the business—like never before. You've learned well. You've gone the extra mile. You're a true five percenter. When ninety-five percenters read this book and understand success like you do, more will turn into five percenters! But I've got to make a phone call now. Will you let me hang on to it? I'll finish reading it and give you a call in a couple of days."

Once again, as usual, I found myself waiting to talk with Zors. I could hardly stand it. But true to his word, two days later he called.

"Jonathan, this is Zors. I have to tell you, this book is right on! The author did a great job. The house on the cover even looks like ours. But I must confess; I don't have the book anymore. Mark Webster stopped by yesterday, and I shared it with him. He read it from cover to cover and loves it. He asked if he could borrow it to share with an old friend of his, Tom Pagano, who is sick and tired of his job—like you used to be before you retired. Tom read *The Parable of the Homemade Millionaire* and he's excited. How can we get more copies of the book?"

Who Is Bryan James?

Bryan James has held management and executive positions in both the finance and healthcare industries for over thirty-five years. He has been president of three different companies that are still active and flourishing today. Bryan is an award-winning salesman, manager, and leader who has been responsible for the professional development of hundreds of people.

He has been recognized, on many occasions, for his outstanding contributions to local charitable organizations and has served on several of their boards of trustees.

Through many years of intense personal research and application, he has refined methodologies that are highly effective in assisting anyone in finding lasting success, happiness, and peace of mind.